Beauty Not
BEHELD

A Daily Guard Against the Lies of Self-Love Culture

Paige Stitt McBride

Foreword by Carl Trueman

Beauty Not Beheld: A Daily Guard Against the Lies of Self-Love Culture

Copyright © 2022 Paige McBride

Published by Hosanna Revival
            4 Kovach Drive, Suite 430
            Cincinnati, OH 45215

Cover design: Hosanna Revival

First printing 2022

Unless otherwise indicated, Scripture quotations are from The ESV® Bible (The Holy Bible, English Standard Version®), copyright © 2001 by Crossway, a publishing ministry of Good News Publishers. Used by permission. All rights reserved.

Scripture quotations marked NIV are taken from the Holy Bible, New International Version®, NIV®. Copyright © 1973, 1978, 1984, 2011 by Biblica, Inc.™ Used by permission of Zondervan. All rights reserved worldwide. The "NIV" and "New International Version" are trademarks registered in the United States Patent and Trademark Office by Biblica, Inc.™

All emphases in Scripture quotations have been added by the author.

Hardcover ISBN: 978-1-954053-16-8

To my sisters, Emily and Grace, and to my dear friend Caelan.

May we all learn to see the world through the eyes of God.

Table of

CONTENTS

Table of

CONTENTS

FOREWORD

Dr. Carl Trueman, PhD

The perennial challenge for the church since at least the time Paul penned 1 Corinthians has been to press the gospel on each generation in a manner which exposes the myths human beings tell each other about themselves and the world in which they live—and to do so in a way that shows how the gospel of Jesus Christ presents us with a better way of living before each other and before God. While that gospel remains the same and will always be foolishness or an offense to whoever happens to be the contemporary equivalent of Paul's Greeks and Jewish critics, the precise ways in which it is dismissed as such are always particular to the cultural ethos of the times.

In an age such as ours, where so-called generation gaps are becoming shorter and shorter in chronological span thanks to the accelerating rate of technological change and its impact upon how we live, that task can seem daunting, especially for those responsible for teaching the younger generation to know, love, and fear the Lord. That is why it is so important to have good material that helps us think through the questions of our day in a manner that is biblical but that also engages directly with the ethos of our day. Paige McBride's devotional is just such a book.

In these pages, Paige takes apart the myth of the modern expressive self, along with the many false beliefs that it fosters: lies about beauty, subjectivism, the authority of emotions, and, underlying them all, the lie that rejects even the possibility of transcendent, absolute truth. Yet she does so in a way that leads the reader gently by the hand, day-by-day, not only to see the futility of the world's conceptions of these matters, but the true beauty of the Bible's answers.

I had the privilege—and delight—of teaching Paige when she was a student. Now our roles have been reversed, and I have had the joy of learning from her via this book; her first, but I earnestly hope not her last. I pray that this volume will have the impact upon the reader that it merits.

Carl R. Trueman
Grove City College
February 2022

A Word On

B E A U T Y

"Women hate their bodies more than ever before," reported skincare company Dove in their 2016 global survey on self-image.[1] The study questioned more than 10,500 women in 13 different countries between the ages of 10 and 60 and concluded that low body-confidence has become—quite literally—a pandemic. Interviewees were convinced that the unrealistic standards in the media are responsible for the issue. They felt that women were under pressure to conform to oppressive and unattainable beauty ideals. Dove was determined to use their platform to fight against these self-demeaning beauty standards and usher in a new age of self-love and body-confidence.

Dove is not the only voice in this movement, nor has the trend shifted since 2016. In fact, in 2021, this topic continues to be the major focus of most female influencers. Powerful women around the globe are banding together to protest these unrealistic standards and are

1   The Dove Global Beauty and Confidence Report, 2016.

calling women to embrace their own definition of beauty. To quote a few among the many:

> "Self-esteem comes from being able to define the world in your own terms and refusing to abide by the judgment of others."[2]
> -*Oprah Winfrey*

> "I love the philosophy of just accepting who you are and just being happy...You define your worth! Don't ever give anyone else that much power over yourself...Less judgment—more dynamic, unbiased self love."[3]
> -*Khloé Kardashian*

> "I have my own definition of what I think is beautiful and sexy."[4]
> -*Selena Gomez*

> "Your self-worth is determined by you. You don't have to depend on someone telling you who you are."[5]
> -*Beyoncé*

2   Oprah Winfrey, "What I Know For Sure." *Oprah.com*, July 19, 2008. https://www.oprah.com/omagazine/what-i-know-for-sure-oprah-winfrey/all, accessed January 5, 2022.

3   Khloe Kardashian, cited by Samantha Schnurr. "Khloe Kardashian Reveals How She Found Self-Love and Acceptance." *E!*, March 14, 2016. https://www.eonline.com/news/748300/khloe-kardashian-reveals-how-she-found-self-love-and-acceptance, accessed January 5, 2022.

4   Selena Gomez, cited by Rachel Heinrichs. "November Cover Star Selena Gomez: 'I Feel in Control.'" *Flare, FashionMagazine.com*, October 1, 2015. https://fashionmagazine.com/flare/november-cover-star-selena-gomez-i-feel-in-control/, accessed January 5, 2022.

5   Beyoncé, cited by Peter Economy. "17 of the Most Inspirational Quotes From Beyonce—Business Genius and Music Superstar." *Inc.com*, June 4, 2019. https://www.inc.com/peter-

The common thread is clear: Largely, culture's response to the conundrum of poor self-image is exhorting women to forget other people's opinions and standards and create their own. In other words, culture wants to remind women, "*Beauty is in the eye of the beholder!* So don't let some beholders get you down, you are the true and only important beholder!" This sentiment sounds empowering at first glance, but the results don't corroborate. Since this study in 2016, the number of voices chanting women's empowerment have grown, and yet so has the number of women who hate the way they look and even hate themselves. Maybe it's time women turn to the Scriptures for their answers instead of their favorite celebrities.

If we really want to debunk all this, we need to get a bit philosophical. Are you ready? I promise I'll be quick. The popular view of beauty today is what philosophers call *aesthetic relativism*. In other words, **beauty is determined by the one perceiving it; it is subjective.** Beauty is believed to be located within the person looking, not within the so-called "beautiful" object. For example, when you gaze at the sunset, beauty is the experience you have as you gaze; it is not an attribute of the sky itself. Beauty is experienced by the *subject* (the person); it is not something in the *object* (the sky). Beauty is not inherent in the sky, it is within your enjoyment of that sky. Therefore, beauty is relative to the person perceiving it; it is subjective beauty, not objective beauty.

economy/17-of-most-inspirational-quotes-from-beyonce-business-genius-music-superstar.html, accessed January 5, 2022.

If beauty is purely subjective, then there is no arguing over what is beautiful and what is not because beauty is only related to personal preference. You cannot argue over preference. By saying beauty is purely subjective—merely a matter of preference— we make it impossible to critically evaluate beauty. If someone says you are ugly, you cannot argue it. You just have to accept that beauty is in the eye of the beholder and this beholder sees none of it in you. But if beauty is objective, then there is open discussion of whether something is beautiful or not. In fact, when someone says that you are not beautiful, you do not have to surrender and say, "Well, beauty is in the eye of the beholder, so I guess they're right." No! An objective beauty allows you to actually argue that you are beautiful even if that person doesn't realize it. You cannot argue over preferences. You can only argue over facts. As long as we insist on subjective beauty, we will make it logically impossible to defend beauty when others do not see it. This is the standard way of thinking about beauty today.

If you Google the definition of beauty this is what you will find: "a combination of qualities, such as shape, color, or form, that *pleases the aesthetic senses*, especially the sight."[6] Dictionary.com defines it this way: Beauty is "the quality present in a thing or person that gives intense *pleasure or deep satisfaction* to the mind, whether arising from sensory manifestations (as shape, color, sound, etc.), a meaningful

---

6   *Google*, s.v. "beauty," accessed January 12, 2022, https://languages.oup.com/google-dictionary-en/. Google's English dictionary is provided by Oxford Languages.

design or pattern, or something else."[7] Finally, Merriam-Webster defines beauty as "the quality or aggregate of qualities in a person or thing that *gives pleasure* to the senses or pleasurably exalts the mind or spirit."[8] What is the common thread in all of these definitions? Beauty is about pleasure. It is about pleasing ourselves. This ideology is not completely misguided; true beauty *does* bring about pleasure. That is why beauty is so powerful. The problem is that we often fail to enjoy that which will ultimately give us the *most* pleasure. Our sinful selves tend to trade in true pleasure and exchange it for a fleeting sense of satisfaction or titillation. So connecting beauty with pleasure is not incorrect, but to only recognize a subjective element in beauty fails to recognize the objective reality of beauty. In fact, we would likely experience a lot more pleasure when confronting beauty if we embraced its objective nature. Unfortunately, most today only understand beauty in subjective terms (what they feel), and therefore, diminish it to only a matter of preference.

What makes this view so appealing to women today is that an experience of beauty can be neither correct nor incorrect, neither right nor wrong. All preferences of beauty are considered equally valid; it is only in arrogance and judgment that someone can say that another should find one object more beautiful than another, let alone one body more beautiful than another! You can't tell people how to feel

---

7   *Dictionary.com*, s.v. "beauty," accessed January 12, 2022, https://www.dictionary.com browse/beauty.

8   *Merriam-Webster*, s.v. "beauty," accessed January 12, 2022, https://www.merriam-webster.com dictionary/beauty.

and what to like, they have the right to their own preferences and opinions. Society's standards and expectations are just the opinions of a few powerful people. However, they should not control you. You can define beauty on your own terms. Beauty is in the eye of the beholder and *you* are the most important beholder in your life. So don't let anyone tell you how to feel when you look in the mirror! This is the type of thinking that dominates our cultural imagination today.

So what's the point of getting all philosophical? Well, this relative definition of beauty sounds great at first—it seems to promise that people cannot impose their view of beauty upon others to shame them—*but* the logical implications of this statement are actually quite troubling. The relative definition of beauty fails to deliver on its promises in three major ways:

Relativism makes beauty and ugliness morally unimportant.

Relativism leads to debilitating narcissism.

Relativism gives people too much power and therefore cannot foster tolerance nor diversity.

1. Relativism makes beauty and ugliness morally unimportant.

If beauty is merely a matter of preference, then so is ugliness. But this makes us more uncomfortable, especially in extreme cases. Most sensible people would agree that morbid images and child pornography are ugly and they would look down on others who find them enjoyable. Why? Because there is something that tells us that the image itself *is* ugly—objectively ugly. It's not a matter of opinion; it's not up for debate. This phenomenon is similar to the case of moral relativism. People are fine with certain moral discrepancies and they will say "you have a right to your opinion" until you say, for example, you believe the Holocaust was morally good. They would respond in anger and proclaim that you are evil, and rightly so. Turns out, they cannot let morality be merely a matter of opinion in every case. So where does the line get drawn between moral issues that are non-negotiable and moral issues which are up for grabs? Similarly, where is the line drawn between which beauty preferences are just matters of opinion and those beauty preferences which are condemnable? Relative beauty does not allow us to evaluate beauty because it makes beauty a matter of mere preference. We cannot condemn anyone's opinion that something is beautiful, because if they find pleasure in it—even if we find it disgusting or repugnant—it is, by their definition, beautiful. You cannot make any judgment calls on a person's beauty preferences. If they like pornography, then it is beautiful and you cannot tell them otherwise. But there comes a point when we are uncomfortable with someone saying that something is beautiful that we *know* is unarguably ugly. We have a deep sense in our hearts that what the person prefers, what that person enjoys, what they find beautiful, is miserably wrong. In fact, we sense that they have committed some sort of sin in enjoying that ugly thing. They might find pleasure in it, but they ought to be shamed for doing so. Just because they enjoy pornographic images of a child, doesn't mean that the images are beautiful. Why do we think that? Because deep down we do have a sense of *objective beauty*. Objective beauty insists that some things are in and of themselves beautiful, and some things are in and of themselves ugly. It is not up for debate (just like the moral evaluation of the Holocaust is not up for debate). If aesthetics become completely relative, completely a matter of opinion, then beauty becomes basically meaningless. Turns out, when we look a little deeper, relative beauty does not fully account for what we know about beauty and ugliness.

2. *Relativism leads to debilitating narcissism.*

The second danger of aesthetic relativism is that it locks you in a cage of self-introspection. It forces you to fixate on yourself because it puts the locus of truth within yourself. Not only is this not biblical, but it allows us to live in the delusion that what we think and feel determines reality. So if you do not like what you see when you look in the mirror, you are ugly. The only way to "be beautiful" is to *see yourself as beautiful*. Beauty itself is not really a thing, it is only the perception of a thing. The only hope for the relativist is to convince themself that what they naturally think is ugly is actually beautiful. They have to force themselves to feel differently when they look in the mirror. This, therefore, leads to a constant focus on the self and its feelings. The task becomes quite worrisome and seemingly hopeless when we try to convince ourselves that every blemish and wrinkle is beautiful. It is an endless cycle of trying to like what we see. Beauty is only there when we feel it, right? Well, we all know that our feelings are like roller coasters. If our body-image is completely dependent on our feelings, it will be forever unstable. We will never win the battle. We will wake up day by day and relive this unstable cycle all over again.

We must be endlessly devoted to *feeling* good about ourselves, because *being* beautiful is equivalent to *feeling* beautiful when beauty is only subjective. Rather than conforming our feelings to reality, we seek to conform reality to our feelings. It's exhausting and sadly ineffective.

3. *Relativism gives people too much power, and therefore, cannot foster tolerance nor diversity.*

Finally, the last issue with relativism is that it cannot deliver on its promises of tolerance and diversity because it grants people the power to define reality. While it might seem nice to be able to define beauty for yourself, relativism does not account for our inordinate craving for acceptance and our deep seated desire to be seen as beautiful and significant. So even if we end up achieving our goal of believing we are beautiful, we are soon empty again because we do not just want to think we are pretty, we want *others* to think we are pretty. And therefore, relativism drags us helplessly into people-pleasing. This may explain why, although women are claiming to only want to be beautiful on their own terms, many girls end up trying to look strikingly similar to the people recognized as beautiful or attractive in the media and by men. We are so desperate to be seen and loved, that we end up conforming. If people determine what is beautiful, we will always end up bowing down to people. If beauty is completely a matter of being seen by other people, then we will not be convinced that we are beautiful until we are seen as such by others. But we know this is not right. A gorgeous, sublime waterfall that has never been seen by one person in all of history is still beautiful. It's beauty is not dependent on being seen. It is beautiful whether or not people notice it. That seems obviously true to us. But a relative definition of beauty gives people all the power when it comes to what is beautiful. And therefore, if no person sees that waterfall and takes pleasure in that waterfall, it is not beautiful. But that can't be right!

For all the empty promises of tolerance and diversity, relative beauty has left us in a culture where women are obsessed with appearance, trends, pictures, and "feeling empowered," and yet are somehow more insecure than ever before. Not only does relativism create philosophical and theological issues, *it does not help*. It may be time to consider a new avenue of action. We need to define beauty biblically. Maybe we will find that the Bible does a better job of making sense of our encounter with beauty than we can.

So this is the conundrum of defining beauty: *We need a definition of beauty that accounts for the inherent quality of beauty in an object* (therefore it is not a matter of opinion and does not depend on people seeing it) but that *also accounts for the fact that beauty is related to individual perception and pleasure in an important way*. In fewer words, it seems right that our definition of beauty has both an objective and a subjective part. It is clear that beauty has something to do with pleasure. But that cannot be the only defining factor, otherwise we will be in the predicament we just spoke of. How can the Bible help us understand beauty as both a matter of fact and a personal experience?

In Genesis 1, God "*saw*" that his creation was good. Notice here, that "good" is not a matter of preference—at least not biblically speaking.

Good and evil aren't matters of opinion. Goodness is an absolute. God perceived something inherently good within his creation; he saw an *objective* good. But it wasn't his "seeing" that made it good. It was good on its own, completely independent of his perception. His "seeing" was just an experience of that good. But we also take note that the verbiage that *"God saw"* connects the goodness of creation with a certain perceptual satisfaction and pleasure. This means that the beauty of the creation and the perception of that beauty are indeed intimately connected. It links the objective quality of beauty in a thing with our enjoyment when encountering it.

Psalm 19 says that "The heavens declare the glory of God" (Psalm 19:1). In this text, creation functions as an instrument of revelation and communication. Created things have a God-ordained way of revealing the greatness of God. Here we find a biblical definition of beauty: *the ability of a thing to communicate truth and/or realize goodness.* A beautiful thing is that which communicates some sort of truth to us or reveals goodness to us in a vivid way. Creation is beautiful because it is a physical form that communicates something true and good about God. And this makes sense of why the human being is "good": the physical form of human beings is an effective communicator of the glory of God. You heard this before: we are his image. A song is rightly called beautiful, because certain sounds and melodies have a way of getting us in touch with transcendence. We cannot put it into words, but we know that the song is beautiful. This definition of beauty is objective, because the ability to reflect truth and goodness is *not* a matter of opinion. You can do it well or poorly. Things can be objectively ugly: they communicate a distortion of God's goodness. It doesn't matter if someone receives pleasure from morbid images, they are condemned in doing so because beauty is not a matter of opinion. The images are not beautiful; they are ugly. And that person looking at them is delighting in that ugliness, which is the essence of sin. So the Bible maintains an objective definition of beauty that makes it meaningful and incredibly important.

But this definition also reminds us that beauty has an essentially communicative role, a perceptual purpose if you will. It is a way to reveal goodness and that is why it gives us so much pleasure. When we consider why people have such a wide variety in what they find beautiful, we realize that this is not because beauty is just a matter of opinion, but that it is because beauty communicates something infinite: God's goodness. Beauty is not just objective, it is transcendentally objective. Therefore, from the many different places and perspectives human beings gaze, they find the glory of God revealed in manifold ways. This accomplishes what relative beauty wants to accomplish: diversity in beauty. When someone sees something truly beautiful that you do not notice, they do not just have a different opinion than you do, they are perceiving a part of the divine goodness that you have yet to enjoy. Therefore, it is an obligation for the Christian to contemplate the beautiful things recognized from different peoples, cultures, and places, for it is our duty to enjoy the manifold glory of our God.

The Christian church cannot be silent on this issue. For many believers, relative beauty has passed off as a "loving" approach, and because of that, many Christians have accepted this movement uncritically; however, a closer look reveals that relative beauty is not loving at all. It is fundamentally anti-biblical, and therefore, it should not surprise us that it has been ineffective. *Aesthetic relativism is not the antidote to our problem of self-image, but more likely the cause of it.* What if the biblical view of objective beauty would provide women with a healthy self-image while also nurturing an environment of true diversity and acceptance among all women? What if we left behind the creed that "Beauty is in the eye of the beholder!" and what if we pursued the Bible's doctrine of a beauty that is not dependent on the eyes of flawed beholders? What if we pursued the courageous mission of perceiving the beauty rarely seen: the beauty not beheld? Let's dive in.

WEEK ONE

The

PERCEIVED

Self

Where It
ALL BEGAN

What They

TELL YOU:

"Beauty is in the eye of the beholder!"

READ GENESIS 1

What God

TELLS YOU:

"So when the woman saw that the tree was good for food, and that it was a delight to the eyes, and that the tree was to be desired to make one wise, she took of its fruit and ate, and she also gave some to her husband who was with her, and he ate."

GENESIS 3:6

If we want to understand identity and beauty in a biblical way, we must start at the very beginning. All throughout the creation narrative, we hear the repetition of God's satisfaction in his handiwork. Each day's creative work is bookended with two repeating statements. They go on as if a drum beat throughout the whole narrative: "And God said..." then "And God saw..." "And God said..." then "And God saw."

First, God's word is creating, and then his eyes are evaluating. In other words, his command brings something out of nothing, and his perception beholds that the "something" is good. Not one creation is made without the command of his word, and not one creation is left without his gaze of affirmation. One design after the next, without fail, we read, "and *God saw* that it was good." This all crescendos on the sixth day as God reflects on the entirety of his work and this time with all the more emphasis. We hear the pattern begin "and *God saw* everything that he had made..." but we are brought to a pause, a breaking of the pattern, and are commanded: *"behold"* (Genesis 1:31).

It is almost as if the author gives us a moment to try to look through the eyes of God so we too can affirm with him in his last evaluation, not just that creation is good, but that it is "very good" (Genesis 1:31). It is an invitation to bask in the creation through the eyes of God. We are offered the opportunity to look and enjoy alongside the King.

We do well to reflect on the importance of these repeated statements. Clearly, Moses wants us to understand something about *God's word* (his creative power) and *his eyes* (his evaluation). Moses wants us to know that they are *authoritative*. Only God can create by his word and evaluate through his eyes. Of course, these are metaphorical ways of illustrating God's power and perception. He does not have a physical mouth to speak words and physical eyes to see things, but these metaphors vividly describe God's authority to create and evaluate. God creates by the authority of his "mouth" and he perceives and evaluates that creation through the authority of his "eyes." This connects God's role as the only Creator to his role as the only Judge. Just as he is the only one with the ability to call things into existence by his word, he is the only one who is ultimately able to judge and declare something "good." Our text wants to pound the phrases, "And God said...And God saw," "And God said...And God saw," "And God said...And God saw" into our minds as if to set the tempo for the following chapters. Because the next time this "said/saw" couplet reappears, there is a new mouth and new set of eyes, neither of which have the authority of God's mouth and God's eyes. Hebrew literature clues you into the significance of an idea by repeating certain phrases or by clearly breaking those established patterns. So it is in Genesis

1 and 3. In chapter 1, we are confronted repeatedly with the God who speaks and sees, and then all of a sudden in chapter 3 we encounter, for the first time, a new voice speaking and a new set of eyes seeing. The authority of the mouth of God is challenged by a new opponent: "*Did God actually say…?*" (Genesis 3:1). The invitation to "behold" alongside God is usurped by a new pair of eyes which see contrary to the eyes of God. This challenge to God's unique ability to create and evaluate is a challenge to his authority. May we carefully consider the consequences of the tempter speaking as though he has the mouth of authority—like the mouth of the God of chapter 1—and a woman who becomes convinced she can authoritatively evaluate things as "good"— like the eyes of the God of chapter 1.

Upon the entrance of this crafty serpent character, it seems as though the tempo set in Genesis 1 and 2 begins to slow down. The song of creation takes an ominous turn. Adam and Eve's ears perceive a new voice as they confront one whose words question the authoritative word of God we remember from Genesis 1. This is our first clue that something is about to go miserably wrong. At first, the woman seems fairly unmoved by the crafty serpent's attempt, but her fall comes swiftly. The slowly fading tempo that began in Genesis 1 comes to a screeching halt and is replaced with a disturbing dissonance. Verse 6 of chapter 3 completes the "said/saw" couplet that was begun by the serpent whose mouth *speaks* contrary to God and concluded by eyes which *saw* contrary to God. The result is a fatal perversion and departure of the original "said/saw" statements of chapter 1: "the woman *saw* that the tree was good for food" (Genesis 3:6), even though this was the very tree God said would bring death (Genesis 2:17).

This is the first time someone other than God "sees" (evaluates) creation. This is significant. We remember the invitation of chapter 1 to "behold" alongside God, but what is alarming here is that Eve's evaluation of the fruit flies directly in the face of God's designation of the tree as dangerous. It is not at all like the invitation in chapter 1 to "behold" as God beholds. Rather, what God saw as bad for Eve, she now *sees* as good. Based on the unauthoritative words of the deceiver, Eve makes what she believes to be an authoritative evaluation of the fruit, rather than accepting God's authoritative word, and submitting her eyes to his vision of the good. Eve refuses the invitation of God in his beckoning call of Genesis 1 to "behold" alongside him and bask in his glory and in what he sees as good. Instead, she resents the opportunity to submit to that which is truly beautiful and attempts to see beauty in the ugly—a fruit that leads to death. In doing so, she begins to define the world *subjectively*. This means that she thinks that she (as the subject) gets to determine the truth. *Truth is dependent on her. She can make it what she wants.* She can decide through her independent evaluation whether or not something is true or false, good or bad. But notice that not only does Eve redefine the true and the good, but she redefines the beautiful: she saw that the fruit was "delightful to the eyes" (Genesis 3:6). By taking aesthetic delight in that which brings about death, Eve is trying to enjoy beauty (revelation of God's glory) in that which is ugly (a distortion of God's glory). This does not mean that the fruit was "ugly" in the sense that it had a malformed physical appearance. The fruit was "ugly" based on it being a conduit of death. And by taking delight in the physical appearance of that which brings death, Eve makes a big mistake. Eve makes beauty a matter of human subjectivism, a matter of preference or opinion, by delighting in a death-bringing fruit in the same way God delighted in his good creation.

While our culture wants to reserve "the beautiful" to a category of opinion and personal conviction, the Bible suggests that the moment we began to see beauty as something we could determine was the very moment we fell into chaos and pain. When Eve thinks her eyes can "delight in" whatever she wants, she makes a serious mistake. And so too, when we think our eyes can "delight in" whatever we want—and so call beautiful whatever we want—we make just as serious a mistake. Whereas the Bible sees this scene as the root of all evil in our world, *our culture might view this scene as a sort of archetypal liberation of the ultimate kind of woman.* American culture teaches us that it is liberating for women to define beauty on their own terms and forsake the oppressive ideals of others. Eve fits the description of the empowered, independent women our culture tends to praise. She does what she wants and defines beauty on her own terms. She will be controlled by no one. She will not be told what is beautiful, not even by God. It is almost as though we coined the saying, "Beauty is in the eye of the beholder!" straight from Genesis 3:6, reading the passage as an affirmation of female empowerment and independence. We tell young girls, "Beauty is in the eye of the beholder!" as a way to boost their self-esteem and teach them confidence and independence, but we make the mistake of Eve. We believe the empty promises of subjectivism. This idea has become so embedded in our cultural perception that often Christians don't even realize its origins in the Garden. Oh, what a pity it is to have culture exalt that which the Bible teaches to be the fundamental disease of humanity!

Genesis 3 describes this spiritual disease in terms of our physical capacity to see. Just as Genesis 1 uses "God saw" as a metaphor for God's authoritative perception of the world, Genesis 3 uses our eyes as a metaphor for our sinful perception of the world. Just as we "see" physical things with perceptual immediacy, we also "see" the world around us with a perceptual immediacy when we evaluate and interpret it. Just as you open your eyes and immediately see without any active decision, so you also are prone to immediately evaluate the world around you and "see" things certain ways. Think of how we use the phrase "I just don't *see* it like that" when we disagree with someone. It means that we do not naturally construe the situation the way they do. By saying we "see" it differently, we mean that we naturally interpret and evaluate it differently. But as the offspring of Eve, we need to understand that we are born wearing defective glasses, seeing the world (naturally and immediately) on our terms, rather than on God's terms. So before we go any further in our discussion of identity and self-image, we must warn ourselves of the danger in the Garden. *We must realize that our perception of things is often misleading: our "eyes" often do not see.* Just like our first mother, we are prone to see that which brings death and *delight* in it. We are prone to see ugliness and call it beauty. Remember the mistake of Eve: The fact that you "see" something as delightful and appealing, does not make it truly beautiful. Just because you feel something, does not make it true. The goal of this devotional is to help us behold that which is truly good and beautiful, as invited to in Genesis 1, and conversely to train our eyes to correct our immediate, mistaken perceptions of the good and beautiful that we inherited from our mother Eve. We have to get back to embracing what God said and saw, instead of trusting what Satan said and what we saw.

REFLECTION & APPLICATION:

1.   *What is a command of God that seems unappealing or unnecessary to you? Find a way to submit and obey that command this week. This is a way to recognize that you do not always "see" the good and beauty that God sees and you trust him enough to do it anyway.*

2.   *Identify one thing in your life that you delight in that God says brings death. Confess and pray for forgiveness.*

3.   *If someone asked you what's wrong with saying that "beauty is in the eye of the beholder," how would you answer?*

Manufacturing

THE SELF

What They

TELL YOU:

"Life is all about finding your authentic self. You decide who you are. Don't let anyone decide for you."

READ GENESIS 3

What God

TELLS YOU:

"But the serpent said to the woman, 'You will not surely die. For God knows that when you eat of it your eyes will be opened, and you will be like God, knowing good and evil.'"

GENESIS 3:4–5

A s we have already discussed, the "said/saw" motif of the creation and fall story clues us into the essence of our sin. Sin concerns how we "see" or "behold" the world. We have considered how this motif teaches us of the perils of *subjectivism* (believing that how we define the world, what is right, good, and beautiful is dependent on the individual's opinion). Now we will consider how Eve actually came to embrace subjective truth. What was the lie that convinced Eve that a system like subjectivism was even possible or, for that matter, good? This question will be our focus in meditating again upon the story of Genesis 3 today. First, we see that the serpent's original tactic to convince Eve of a world of subjective truth seemed fairly ineffective. He asks, *"Did God actually say...?"* (Genesis 3:1). But his questioning of God's command is not enough to sway her. She responds to the doubting serpent by correcting his lies (Genesis 3:2-3). She appears to be fairly unmoved by his schemes. But her firmness does not last long. It only took a handful of words to completely fog her clarity on God's word and God's goodness. What exactly was the lie that had the power to allure a woman already living in paradise? It was a lie about her identity—an identity that she was given in Genesis 1.

Eve was the image of God (Genesis 1:27). She and Adam had the privileged role among all the other creatures—to be walking, talking reflections of their Creator. While all of creation sang God's glorious praise by realizing his eternal power and divinity (Romans 1:20), human beings were the only creation granted such a prestigious status as God's very image. What is an image? An image is something that represents a reality. It is a reflection of something or a portrayal of something. So as the image of God, we are his representatives, those who are made to reflect and portray him on the earth. The declaration that humankind is the image of God means that we cannot understand "the self"—our identity—apart from its proper relationship to God because we were made to reflect and represent him. Therefore, to "know yourself" necessitates first that you know how you relate to God. If we are the image of God, then in some sense it is more important that we understand who God is than who we are because we cannot reflect something we don't know. Being the "image of God" means that *the self is essentially dependent*. It must go outside of itself to define itself. It cannot find meaning only by looking inward. And it will make no sense of itself if it insists on obscuring that which it is dependent upon. In other words, if we persist in our ignorance of God, we cannot make sense of the "self" because to be a "self" is to be the image *of God*. It is only in remembering humanity's God-given identity that we can understand the danger of Satan's temptations in Genesis 3:5. Eve's identity was to be defined by her purpose: She was to communicate something about who God is by being his image. She was made to point to another. It was only in fulfilling this purpose that she would flourish.

Knowing this, in his second attempt at deceiving Eve, the serpent tries to distort the goodness of Eve's designated identity as God's image. This time around, he does not even deny the fact that God forbids the fruit (like he originally did in verse 1); instead, the snake dangles a false identity in front of Eve as if her God-given one was insufficient or inadequate. In doing so, he insinuates that God has hidden intentions behind forbidding the fruit. He admits that God did indeed say to not eat the fruit, but it was only because God knows that "when you eat of it your eyes will be opened, and *you will be like God*, knowing good and evil" (Genesis 3:5). Instead of questioning God's commands like his first attempt, he questions God's goodness. He makes God look like the bad guy. He wants Eve to take hold of a new theology, one in which God is seen as capricious and selfish, withholding that which is truly good from his creation. Apparently, the role he gave them as image-bearers was not generous at all, it was a scheme to keep them from becoming his equals. According to the serpent, God's commandments were the way in which God suppressed Eve's full potential to be just like him. He could keep his unique superiority by forcing Eve to follow his rules. So the serpent reveals Eve's "full potential," she can be just like God. How can Eve be just like God? Remember who has the authority to define what is "good" in chapter 1 of Genesis? God alone. So now, the way Eve can assert a God-like status is to be the arbiter of what is "good." She believed *she* could "see" and determine certain things to be good, just like God did in chapter 1. It was this allure of self-exaltation—her ability to be like God—that took Eve: hook, line, and sinker.

She likely still remembered that God said not to eat the fruit, but now she does not see God as one with her best interests in mind, but as one who restrains her from reaching self-actualization. The reality of God's command is powerless when her vision of the Commander is warped in this way. And not only does she take on this new theology, she adopts a new anthropology—a new view of humanity. When she is confused about the identity of God, she is also confused about her own identity. She no longer associates man's identity as one that reflects God's image, but instead sees mankind as competing for God's role and status. *She ceased to believe she was who God said she was and began believing she could be whatever she wanted to be.* The devil, in one foul swoop, has convinced Eve to believe lies about God and herself in order to secure her disobedience. She rejects her essentially dependent identity as God's image for an identity she can engineer on her own. For Eve, in that moment, God and his commands seemed uncompelling. Even worse, they seemed to her to be the enemy to her most "authentic self." The self who can be like God is essentially independent and autonomous, and can define good and evil. God's authority was now the obstacle she had to tear down to establish her own authority. And while she may have thought she was stepping into freedom and empowerment, she had actually just secured her demise.

What is most relevant for our discussion on identity and current cultural trends is that the moment Eve accepted a subjective definition of the self, she lost herself (*even* if she had a deceptive feeling of finding herself). In non-philosophical terms, Eve believed that she could determine who she was. *She believed that she could define her identity.* She believed she could be like God, even when God had already given her a definitive designation, not as God, but as his image. In pride, she trades the paradise of being God's reflection for a lie that tells her she can be whoever and whatever she wants to be. In other words, she embraced "her truth" instead of *the* Truth. She "finds herself" by looking within and disregarding the standards and labels of another. Is this starting to sound familiar? It is the typical advice you would get today if you face an identity crisis of any kind. People tell you to look within, to focus on yourself, and to ignore any outside expectations of who you ought to be. But this very advice is a continuation of the original mistake of Eve.

When we try to construct our identities on our own (independent of God), we demonstrate exactly what sin has done to us: We think we can decide who we are, and when we do that, we believe ourselves to be God. We think we can take on his role as the ultimate "see-er" of the world, defining what is good, beautiful, and right, and what it means to be a self. And that is not just a shift in theology, anthropology, nor philosophy, *it is the epitome of arrogance.* Be weary when you hear people say "You can be whoever you want to be!" for they do not realize what they do when they make such a proclamation. Genesis would have us think twice before we buy the lie that there is freedom and empowerment in defining yourself on your own terms. Behind such a belief is a mistaken theology and an arrogant view of humanity. And not only that, but behind such beliefs are empty promises. They are a ploy of the deceiving serpent. He wanted Eve to think self-creation was good for her. But that was merely a trick. Self-creation did not lead her to freedom, it led her to shame. If we learn from Eve, we must affirm that independence is not the mark of a true woman. True womanhood is rooted in being God's image—an essentially dependent identity. If we want to think of ourselves in healthy ways, we must start with this crucial recognition: we are not God, we are his image. And that is *good*.

REFLECTION & APPLICATION:

1.   *Can you think of a time you disobeyed God because you thought you were "missing out" on something? How are you making the same mistake as Eve when you do that? Remember, our disobedience denies not only the commands of God, but the goodness of God.*

2.   *Why does understanding who God is help us understand who we are?*

3.   *The greatest mistake of identity is to think we can define ourselves however we like. Why is that true? Can you think of ways that you try to define yourself apart from God?*

All Eyes

ON ME

What They

TELL YOU:

"Never be ashamed of who you are!"

READ GENESIS 3

What God

TELLS YOU:

*"Then the eyes of both were opened, and they
knew that they were naked. And they sewed fig
leaves together and made themselves loincloths."*

GENESIS 3:7

Today we continue on in our careful trek through the story of creation and the fall. We have considered God's authoritative word and evaluation in Genesis 1 and we have seen that thwarted in Satan's word and Eve's evaluation in Genesis 3. We have realized the dangerous business of subjectivism—particularly, its danger when it comes to defining beauty subjectively and its danger when it comes to defining the self subjectively. We can now begin to connect the dots between the sin of subjectivism (defining things however we want to) and our current state as human beings. Directly following the description of Eve's turn toward subjective truth and the rebellion that it entailed in verse 6, verse 7 describes the immediate consequence: *"and they knew that they were naked"* (Genesis 3:7). This crude statement now describes the standard condition of humanity in all of history. Remembering the emphasis on God "seeing" things in Genesis 1, when we read the much-dreaded words that Eve "saw" something contrary to God's word, we anticipate something huge. We wonder if the couple will drop dead instantly after their first bite. Afterall, God did say that the day they eat of it they will surely die (Genesis

2:17). Instead, the result of verse 7 seems rather anticlimactic. They don't drop dead, they just realize they are naked. But what does that really mean? We would expect that Adam and Eve were not physically blind nor were they stupid before their rebellion. We would assume they could acknowledge that their skin was uncovered. So what is this realization of nakedness? What's the big deal?

In actuality, this reality in verse 7 is much more dramatic than we might first think. In this very moment, as Adam and Eve grasp their nakedness, they are introduced to self-consciousness for the first time. And this new *sense of self* demands to be acknowledged. It cannot be ignored. Adam and Eve are suddenly held captive in their subjectivity. They cannot deny this debilitating sense of self. And this sense of self is the revelation that they are *exposed*. They know they are being seen—and not in a good light. They feel vulnerable, embarrassed and humiliated. They want to be covered up. They want to hide. The immediate result of their sin was a crippling sense of what we know as *shame*. Their shame is the awareness that they are being "seen" in a bad way. They wanted to "see" things however they pleased, and now they cannot bear being "seen" by each other and their God. Their assertion of independence has led their minds to be dominated by their sense of self. The author wants to make an explicit connection between the manufacturing of their own truth/identity and their feeling of shame.

Our culture has a similar fixated obsession over our "sense of self." Many today think the essence of life is a journey of "finding ourselves," of "self-realization." We tend to think that the day we come to know ourselves most authentically will be the day we have achieved freedom and joy, life to the fullest. And so we focus on ourselves and prioritize ourselves to tap into our true self. Self-awareness and self-knowledge become the key to a good life. But it is interesting that the Bible seems to associate self-consciousness with sin. It's as if, before eating the fruit, Adam and Eve lived in a blissful state of self-forgetfulness, of self-*un*awareness. This would not mean that they did not know that they were "a self," they certainly had a sense of self, an identity. They knew they were a self, but didn't have to think too much about it. Think about when parts of our body are working properly. They do not draw much attention towards themselves. If your foot is doing a good job at being a foot, you don't really notice it. But once your foot malfunctions, suddenly, it's the only thing you're paying attention to. It's not that before your injury you didn't realize the existence of your foot; it's just that when your foot does what it's supposed to do, it doesn't demand non-stop attention. But when your foot isn't functioning properly, it constantly begs for attention. So too, when our identity is functioning properly, it doesn't usually demand constant recognition and attention.[1] But when our identity is bruised, it becomes a fragile ego that always needs to be noticed and coddled. The insight from Genesis 3:7 is this: The moment Adam and Eve began to fixate on themselves was actually the moment they entered into shame. Their assertion of subjectivism actually led to an inescapable focus on the subject. They were caged in self-absorption.

1   This illustration is from Timothy Keller, found in his book *The Freedom of Self Forgetfulness: The Path to True Christian Joy* (LaGrange, KY: 10Publishing, 2021), pg 15-16.

Subjectivism and independence from God was not their path to freedom, but to their bondage to sin. Self-awareness had led them to a state of disgrace in which they ran and hid from that which was good—God—because of fear of exposure for what they truly were—no longer good.

This entrance of self-consciousness illuminates what exactly the biblical term shame describes. It relates not just to a poor sense of self, but also to the recognition of others' seeing you as that self. It is a feeling that all eyes are on you and you are exposed for what you truly are. It is a crippling sense of the condemning eyes of God or humanity upon you. This is the essence of shame. *It is the feeling that you are being seen or exposed in a bad light.* We know the feeling. It's not a foreign, ancient idea. This is our daily life. For many of us, it is what we dread most in our world. Notice, though, that shame is first an embarrassment before God. Because of the manipulative and evil ways humans treat one another, one can often be haunted by an unwarranted sense of shame. If someone is treated with disregard and complete disrespect, as if they weren't the image of God, they take on a ruined sense of self. They begin to think they deserve to be treated poorly and that they are not worthy of dignity. This is what I will call victim-shame. The person is truly a victim of their shame. This type of shame is to be corrected. This kind of shame is anti-gospel. But the shame Adam and Eve felt, what I will call sin-shame, was perfectly warranted and not to be corrected. We can understand this by considering the phrase that comes before their realization of their nakedness. Genesis 3:7 says, "and their eyes were opened and they knew they were naked." This insinuates that this revelation that they were naked was a true one. It came from eyes that were working as they should. Their eyes were "opened." They "saw" something true this time, and it was their nakedness. The shame they were feeling as they realized their nakedness was not improper. It was spot on. God did not respond to Eve saying, "What are you doing hiding in that bush?! Get out here, you have nothing to be ashamed of!" Instead, God beckons them to come out from hiding, *not because they shouldn't feel guilty for their sin, but because he is gracious*. But despite seeking confession from the couple, God just gets excuses. Consequently, he condemns the couple and the serpent. And in this way, he affirms their sense of shame as appropriate. What they did is worthy of punishment, and therefore, worthy of shame.

From here on out, the Bible uses nakedness as a symbol of shame, exposure, and humiliation. This might provide us an insight for our current day and age. Our sexually-liberated culture might advise Adam and Eve to forget the fig leaves, they don't need to cover up! We even might read this passage and think that clothing is just a result of the fall so we don't need to wear it. But before we interpret Genesis as saying that we shouldn't wear clothes, let us look at how God responds to their nakedness. He does not tell them to ditch the fig leaves and celebrate their bodies. He doesn't advise "body-confidence" in that sense. Rather than getting rid of their covering, God actually provides a *more* thorough covering for Adam and Eve, insinuating that their covering for their shame was inadequate; they needed something more. Their nakedness needed to be covered. If they hadn't done anything wrong, there would be no need for a covering. But God condemns the couple and shows that they are going to need a better covering for their mistake than a fig leaf. To deny Adam and Eve's need for clothing would be to deny their need for atonement.

So recognizing the inadequacy of a few leaves to cover their sin, God makes a gracious (and bloody) provision of clothing for the couple. He uses the skins of an animal to clothe them. A sufficient covering for their shame required blood to be spilled; a plant would not do. An animal's blood was shed on their behalf for a satisfactory covering of their shame. This act is a glimpse of God's grace and provision for sinners in their shame. Indeed, it is a picture of what would become the entire economy of salvation: substitutionary atonement. Something would shed its blood in place of humanity in order to atone for their shame. God would not say, "no need to be ashamed!," but God would say, "Be ashamed of what you've done, and be astounded at how I will atone for it. Watch me make something glorious out of something shameful." Therefore, just as nakedness is a biblical symbol of shame, clothes are a biblical symbol of salvation. They are a reminder of God's grace towards his wayward people. He is a God who makes a provision to account for our mistakes, even when we don't deserve it. Does your clothing reflect a God who graciously covers our shame and gives us life, or does it reflect a mistaken sense of empowerment that has nothing to be ashamed of? Did you ever think that your clothing could be a reflection on your salvation? Don't deny the reality of your sin-shame. Acknowledge it and allow your clothing to be a daily reminder that God provides a covering for us when our sin exposes us. That is the gospel.

REFLECTION **&** APPLICATION:

1.   *Shame is ultimately caused by our rebellion against God, not by low self-esteem. Do you ever dismiss a feeling of shame because you think it is just low self-esteem, when in reality it is because you know you have failed to live as God has commanded?*

2.   *Shame is appropriate for the sinner. We should feel shame before a holy God. Think of a situation in which you should feel shame (an example of sin-shame). Think of a situation in which your sense of shame should be corrected (victim-shame).*

3.   *The gospel is all about covering our shame so that we no longer have to hide before God. Therefore, clothing can be a symbol of salvation. How can you make your clothing reflect that truth, instead of being about exalting yourself and showing off?*

Always

THE VICTIM

What They

TELL YOU:

"You deserve better."

READ GENESIS 3

What God

TELLS YOU:

*"He said, 'Who told you that you were naked? Have you eaten
of the tree of which I commanded you not to eat?' The man said,
'The woman whom you gave to be with me, she gave me fruit
of the tree, and I ate.' Then the Lord God said to the woman,
'What is this that you have done?' The woman said, 'The serpent
deceived me, and I ate.'"*

GENESIS 3:11-13

W e have learned that the story of the fall has some crucial lessons for us to learn about truth and selfhood. We have seen that the fall of humanity consisted, in large measure, brought about a twisted sense of self. We have reflected on the ways we ought to think of ourselves, while also exposing the ways we tend to think of ourselves. We have considered how sin leads immediately to self-consciousness, a perception of the self that we are exposed. Therefore, our sense of self is often dominated by shame, and that is not necessarily wrong. Now we must investigate one final tendency of our self-perception revealed in Genesis 3: *victimhood*. It is a self-perception that pushes back against the true self-perception of shame. When Adam and Eve originally experience shame, they have a sense that they are responsible for their actions. They are recognizing that they have done something wrong. That's why they feel ashamed. And so they run and hide. This is subconscious acknowledgement of their accountability before God. It is a recognition of the validity of their shame. They know that they ought to be punished for what they have done, that's why they hide. But they soon experience a contradictory spirit of pride that leads them to claim innocence and blame shift, as if they weren't culpable at all.

This scene quickly proves that the new self-understanding Adam and Eve have adopted is quite dysfunctional. First they run and hide in shame, acknowledging that they are responsible for their disobedience. But then upon questioning, they attempt to claim some sort of innocence. For the man, it was the woman who made him eat; he can hardly be held responsible for her mischief! Better yet, it was the woman that God gave him. Maybe God should share some of the blame here! As for Eve, without the option of blaming her partner in crime (literally), she reminds God that the serpent deceived her. She was duped. Just innocently confused! After all, didn't we mention that he was the "most crafty" of all the beasts?! So in response to the God-given opportunity to take responsibility and confess, Adam and Eve scramble before their Judge and revert to blame shifting, despite their deep felt sense of shame and accountability. This new sense of self has led them into a contradiction. They cannot deny the reality of the shame they feel, and yet they want to claim that they have not messed up in any serious way. They refuse to allow their shame to produce confession, as it should. Instead, they persist in contradiction, as they plead innocence while still too embarrassed of their nakedness to come out from behind the trees. The lies (their pride) and the truth (their shame) are fighting for dominance and right now their pride is winning.

Instead of humbly confessing before their God and Judge, Adam and Eve are satisfied with pointing their fingers at each other, the serpent, and even at the Judge himself. But their denial of shame is not met with the expected freedom from its power. After condemning the serpent, who of course is also held responsible in the eyes of the Just Judge, God condemns the couple. Their blame shifting has done them no good, they are guilty nonetheless. *Their denial of reality has no power to change the reality. Their denial of shame has no power to cure their shame.* But in his persistent grace, God gives a glimpse of hope for the couple and their legacy in humanity. Though they continue to avoid the recognition of their shame, God recognizes it and seeks to cover it. Their nakedness is not to be ignored, it is to be covered. Sadly, Eve and her children will continually try to point the finger, grasping at every opportunity to prove another person guilty and themselves innocent. But God will soon set up a system of reminder, where they daily learn to acknowledge their responsibility and quit pointing the finger. A system where they can cover their shame through the substitutionary blood-shedding of animals in the temple. The aroma of sacrifice was not just a pleasing aroma to the Lord, but was a constant reminder to the people that they are responsible for their mistakes and yet God has made a way to forgive them. They are to consistently call back to God's original provision for his guilty children. They are not to avoid their responsibility and guilt, but they are to rest in his grace towards those who do confess. All this, of course, foreshadows the ultimate clothing of the naked through the precious blood of Christ Jesus who, though he was not guilty, would bear the shame of the guilty, that they might experience the justification of the godly.

It is important that we understand the ways in which our culture teaches us to perceive ourselves. We must fight for awareness of the assumptions and beliefs that dominate our surroundings, because it turns out that there is nothing new under the sun. The lies that Adam and Eve believed in the garden are alive and well in America today (and around the world, for that matter), just in new forms. Self-love culture teaches us that we just need more love and attention. We just need to give ourselves grace and celebrate our flaws. We preach to ourselves that we deserve better from the world around us. But the Christian must fight to see herself in truth. And this means that she cannot primarily see herself as a victim. Ultimately, she is not a victim of the world around her. Her participation in rebellion against God has made the world the way it is. She is responsible for her mistakes. She will be held accountable. And if she cannot let go of her victim-identity, she will never grasp the gospel. Only when she realizes that she has a debt to pay will she realize the great love of the One who paid it in her place.

REFLECTION & APPLICATION:

1. When we sin, God seeks confession from us. Try offering a prayer of confession. It is a way to fight your victim mindset and acknowledge your accountability before God. Not only that, but it is a way to remind yourself that your God loves to forgive those who confess. Try to incorporate confession into your daily life.

2. Can you think of situations in your life where you only focused on how other people messed up, instead of admitting your part in the situation?

3. What is a victimhood mindset and why does a victimhood mindset ruin our relationship with God and others?

Affirmation

HUNGRY

What They

TELL YOU:

"You are worthy of love and affirmation."

READ PSALM 32

What God

TELLS YOU:

*"I acknowledge my sin to you and I did not cover my iniquity;
I said 'I will confess my transgressions to the LORD,' and you
forgave the iniquity of my sin."*

PSALM 32:5

The Psalms are the believer's emotive toolbook. The psalter acknowledges the many extreme emotions that take hold of us and then provides a framework through which believers can work through those feelings and perceptions. Because of this, the psalms provide us with lots of wisdom when it comes to self-perception and even self-talk. Whereas popular opinion would tell you that self-talk is about building confidence and affirming yourself, the self-talk found within the psalms seems more occupied with the truth, questioning the self when it forgets the truth (Psalm 42:5), and often commanding the self to embrace the truth (Psalm 103:1-2). As it turns out, modern psychology and feminist movements were not the first ones to consider the value of self-talk. The book of Psalms offers us a biblical way of thinking through our emotions and talking back to them. Psalm 32:5 is a particularly intriguing example of self-talk. David recalls a situation in which he was bogged down by his sin and gives us a quick inside view of the conversation that was going on within himself through it all. The psalm begins with David's declaration of the blessings of forgiveness. He basks in the freedom and security that comes with the knowledge of good standing before God (Psalm 32:1-2). But then he backstracks to give us some context. His appreciation of God's forgiveness only came after he learned a hard lesson about facing his sin. He remembers a time when he repressed the presence of his sin. He kept silent about it. He did not confess it. It is almost as if David took the conventional wisdom of our day for those who struggle with low self-esteem: "Don't beat yourself up, give yourself grace; you don't have to focus on all your flaws! Your imperfections are not a problem, you are perfectly imperfect!" This is a typical example of the self-talk that is encouraged today. It emphasizes our need for affirmation rather than confrontation.

And so David kept silent, apparently under the impression that his sin did not need to be acknowledged, let alone focused upon. But as he persisted in his avoidance technique, he was burdened by an equally persistent pain. His bones seemed as though they were wasting away. He groaned all day long. His strength had dried up (32:3-4). Why? Because day and night *God's hand was heavy upon him.* Despite his efforts to forget about his guilt, the shadow of the righteous Judge of humanity follows him day and night. The fact that David locates the source of his pain in the heavy hand of God suggests that this experience of physical and spiritual suffering was a manifestation of sin-shame, the kind of shame that feels the burden of God's presence and one's exposure before it. It was the kind of shame that led the guilty to hide in the bushes in Genesis 3. They were aware of the holy presence of God, and felt uncomfortable before him due to their rebellion. David's experience is likely comparable. David feels this shame because, despite trying to ignore his sin, he cannot ignore the feeling that God sees what he has done. It is in this context that we read the conversation inside David's head in verse 5: "I said, 'I will confess my transgression to the LORD.'" David decides to try a new kind of self-talk. A self-talk that pushes him to confront the truth. David takes a new route concerning his sin, guilt, and shame. Instead of keeping silent, he is going to fess up. This is the turning point that enables him to proclaim the original joys of verses 1 and 2.

David's decision in verse 5 to acknowledge his shame before God might sound like negative self-talk to us. Our contemporary conscience may be a bit offended, thinking "You have nothing to be ashamed of!" But for David, and I will argue for us all, this strategy of confession (that we might reject as oppressive and depressive) works awfully well. It is by confession that David can move into freedom and praise. His first exclamations of joy are totally dependent upon his prior confession and confrontation with the reality of his shame. *It was the avoidance of his shame that kept him from joy, not the recognition of it.* This speaks to the powerful ways in which forgiveness (and therefore, the gospel) works. When David refused to acknowledge his sin and shame, he could not enjoy the blessings of forgiveness. Therefore, forgiveness is therapeutic because it meets our true needs, not avoids our true needs. It acknowledges the weight of our shame and compensates for it. This means that the joy and freedom of the gospel is dependent upon the recognition of our shame. But the popular view in our current society is to *deny our need of forgiveness* and *emphasize our need of affirmation.* This emphasis reveals a non-biblical view of the self in which our true illness is not an offense against a holy God, but is a deficiency in the love, affirmation, or significance we believe we need and are worthy of. You can see how this connects to the victimhood mentality.

But the Bible recognizes both your need for forgiveness and your desire for love and acceptance. David understands the power of shame firsthand, and wants to share with his audience the most effective way of handling it. Psalm 32 gives us the dos and don'ts of shame-coping. His first strategy, suppression and avoidance, fails miserably. He could not seem to lose a pervasive sense of discomfort within himself. Sound familiar? Culture gives us a lot of "empowering" tips and tricks to avoid the feeling of shame, but they usually don't deliver fully on their promises. Maybe for a short time, but rarely long term. It seems most of us just cannot shake the sense of shame that haunts us. It doesn't matter how much we affirm ourselves with positive self-talk or even if others shower us with affirmation, shame continues to be a problem for us. So David says no to shame-denial and yes to shame-recognition. He says goodbye to ignoring his need for forgiveness and says hello to the joy of being pardoned. He stops insisting on the "positive self-talk" that only affirms himself, and starts accepting the fact that he ought to be punished for his sins.

Self-love culture would have you think that affirmation is the center of the gospel. When we scroll through our social media feeds, the prominent message on many Christian accounts is affirmation-based: "You are loved," "You are worthy," "You are beautiful," "You are enough." By emphasizing this, we have turned the gospel into a self-esteem project instead of an atonement project. And we have done this by convincing ourselves that our deepest problem as a human being is a lack of self-love, self-confidence, self-appreciation, self-care, self-this, and self-that. So if that is where we locate our greatest needs, in order for the gospel to be relevant, we turn it into a self-esteem boost. The main message of the gospel becomes "you are affirmed," rather than "you are redeemed." But as we have seen in Genesis 3, the real problem of humanity is our guilt and shame before God. We have disobeyed God and face punishment for it. We have failed to image him as we were made to and now we have a deep sense of humiliation and embarrassment. The reality of our sin (guilt) and the sense of self that comes with it (shame) are our true problem. And that's why the gospel is about justification (declaring the guilty as innocent) and glory (the transformation of shame). The gospel is this: *God finds a way to justify the guilty so that he can glorify the ashamed.* But if we do not accept the pressing reality of our guilt and our shame, then we cannot see the gospel as Scripture would have us see it.

When we resist the reality of shame and try to convince ourselves we are not in need of forgiveness but only of affirmation, we suffer two consequences. First, we feel the heaviness of God's righteousness upon us as David did. We keep silent in regard to our sins and so we waste away. We groan in confusion, wondering why our sense of self continues to be a burden to us. And second, the gospel fails to meet our (supposed) needs. We find the Scriptures unhelpful when we insist that God is the vending machine that doles out affirmation and self-confidence boosts. The Bible starts seeming irrelevant and we end up reading self-help books instead of Scripture. David would have us do otherwise. He knows that the gospel of forgiveness is what we really need. No, the gospel does not always affirm you. It does not always say you are enough. It does not always say you are worthy. Rather, the gospel affirms Jesus and says he is enough and he is worthy. Rather than avoiding our shame, let us, alongside King David, bask in the reality of a God who is quick to forgive and atone for our sins and our shame.

REFLECTION & APPLICATION:

1. The way to cope with shame is to confess our sins, not make light of them. Sometimes we need to be rebuked, not celebrated. Can you think of a time when you went looking for affirmation but you really just needed correction?

2. How can we acknowledge shame that is caused by our sins? What is a healthy way to do that? What are some ways you try to avoid your feelings of shame? How can you change that?

3. What is an example of biblical self-talk when we are dealing with sin-shame (shame that comes from our disobedience)? How might self-talk differ when we are dealing with victim-shame (shame that comes when someone wrongfully treats us without dignity and respect)? When do we need "negative self-talk" and when do we need "positive self-talk"? Think of ways that self-talk can end up being a way to preach yourself the gospel daily on repeat.

Comparison:

THE GAME OF LIFE

What They

TELL YOU:

*"Never be ashamed of showing off and being proud of your body
and your accomplishments. You should celebrate who you are."*

READ 1 CORINTHIANS 13

What God

TELLS YOU:

*"Love is patient and kind; love does not envy
or boast; it is not arrogant."*

1 CORINTHIANS 13:4

We have seen how the fall of humanity took place within the realm of self-image. We have explored all the mistaken perceptions of the self that have come with the Fall. We have broken down the many different ways in which we perceive ourselves incorrectly, including our perception of beauty, our attempt to make ourselves something that we are not, and our insisting that we are the victim instead of the criminal. But there is one last piece of the puzzle when talking about our sinful perception of the self. Not only did the fall ruin our self-perception, but it also distorted our perception of other "selves." Just as we adopt a crooked view of ourselves, we also take on a crooked view of our fellow image-bearers.

This leads us to one of the most famous passages in all of Scripture: I Corinthians 13. It is a marvelous description of the heart of Christian ethics: love. Amidst controversy concerning the use of spiritual gifts in public worship, Paul completes his advice to the Corinthian church with a reminder of priority. As he speaks of the diversity of gifts within the body—where some are apostles, some teachers, some work

miracles, some administrate, some serve, and some speak in tongues—
he calls the Corinthian church to remember a "more excellent" way
than all of these gifts (1 Corinthians 12:31). Without this one thing,
the flashy spiritual gifts of the Corinthians turn out to be nothing.
And this "more excellent way" is the way of love. The Christian life,
according to Paul, is primarily a life about love. And no matter what
else you do or what else you have, if you do not love, you do not know
the Christian life.

Our culture eats up the Christian emphasis on love. It is one of the
parts of Christianity that scratches our cultural itches. And in a lot
of ways, the popular cultural emphasis on kindness, compassion, and
love is a wonderful aspect of contemporary culture. But it also has
its issues. We are also a needy society when it comes to how we view
ourselves. We tend to think of ourselves in terms of needs, rather than
duties (which is a rather new view of the self historically). We tend
to emphasize all the things we deserve, rather than our obligations.
Because of this, we can sometimes interpret the Scripture's call to
love in a distorted way. We make life about fulfilling our desire for
attention, significance, and affirmation, and justify that by saying
the gospel is all about love. But we fail to realize Paul's definition of
love in 1 Corinthians 13, not to mention Jesus' example of love. Let's
take a look.

There are so many treasures of wisdom found in this short, dense
passage. But today we focus on verse 4's claim that love cannot
coincide with envy, boasting, or arrogance. Defining envy will be key

to understanding the standards of love and the mistakes we make in our perception of other people. *Envy is the disposition to view other people and their qualities or possessions in terms of competition.* More specifically, you see everything in terms of *you*. When you see a beautiful girl, you don't just think, "She is beautiful." You think, "She is more beautiful *than me*." When you see someone with good style, you don't just think, "She has good style," you think, "She has better style *than me*." Envy means that you see people based on how they compare to you, and therefore, *envy is an essentially self-absorbed worldview.* You become jealous of other people's qualities and possessions because you build your sense of self around how you stack up next to others. Your self-esteem and self-worth is a ranking game, and therefore, someone else's win becomes your loss. And because of this you begin to despise others who have a quality or possession that you lack. The fact that you are less beautiful than the girl means that her beauty is a problem for you rather than something you can enjoy and celebrate. The fact that you do not have as many cute outfits as that girl means that she bothers you rather than inspires you.

Do you see how envy is anti-love? Envy cannot coincide with love because it insists on seeing another person's gain as your deficit. Envy perceives the other in terms of how they threaten or benefit *me*. Love perceives the other in terms of how I might threaten or benefit *them*. Envy sees people in light of competition and status, while love sees people in light of solidarity and companionship. Envy is the loathing of the good of another. Love is the desire for the good of another. All the more, the Christian notion of love goes beyond merely wanting and celebrating the good of another, but Christian love often sacrifices some good for itself in order to achieve a good for the other. Christ did not consider his own good when he died on the cross. His motivation was the good of the other. Therefore, *Christian love is essentially others-oriented*. It is essentially selfless, which is why it clashes with envy, which is essentially selfish. Biblical love says the world is not about me. Self-love says I need the world to be about me. And similarly, envy says everyone in the world is a competitor for me. People become objects who either boost or hinder our pride. People's qualities and achievements are seen in terms of how they help or hurt our own sense of self. This tendency towards comparison was seen in the Corinthians as they tried to one-up each other with cooler spiritual gifts and possibly ostracize those who did not have certain flashy, spiritual gifts. Paul fights back against their culture of comparison, saying it cannot thrive while love thrives. Envy and love are mutually exclusive; they cannot flourish together. At the root of a culture of comparison is a culture of self-absorption which contradicts love. Love cannot envy.

We can even see the embryonic beginnings of envy in the fall. Rather than embracing her call as the image of God, Eve saw an opportunity to increase her comparative ranking. She was not satisfied with imaging God; she wanted to *be* God. She despised her role of inferiority. She started seeing the world in terms of who-has-what and who-doesn't-have-what and she connected that to her sense of self. Rather than delighting in God's unique greatness and superiority, she saw it as a threat to her own happiness. Her position beneath the authority and rule of God became a threat to her identity and security. But in reality, God's kingship and exclusive deity were the glue that held together her identity and her security. Ever since Eden, we have continued to see God and people in that same light. Envy plays an essential role in our sinful state.

What might this mean for the church today? It means that we must be wary of self-love culture because it fosters self-absorption which fosters envy which ultimately contradicts love. In other words, self-love culture insists that we focus on ourselves and see ourselves as the priority and that is, quite simply, the opposite of the biblical definition of love. We are not to see others as a threat to our identity. We are to see our ability to love others as a part of our identity because being made in the image of God means we are made to *love*—not just *be loved*. This has a very practical application. Our culture encourages boasting, especially when it takes the form of showing off our bodies. It is praised as a form of self-confidence and empowerment. But we must remember that boasting and arrogance are the offspring of envy. And all of these are contrary to love. If we do want to always be compared to others, let's not give other women more opportunities to compare themselves to us. "Showing off" is not loving, it is the fruit of an envious heart that wants to assert it's ranking above others. Love does not envy and love does not boast.

REFLECTION & APPLICATION:

1. *When we view ourselves in the wrong way, we end up viewing other people in the wrong way. Can you think of examples in your life of how you view other people in terms of how they stack up to you?*

2. *Envy means that you base your self-worth on comparison. We need to stop seeing other people as our competitors and start seeing them as our companions. How might we do this?*

3. *Don't buy the lie that self-confidence and self-celebration are innocent forms of self-expression. Can you think of ways on social media that boasting is trendy and often celebrated, causing us to reinforce a harmful sense of identity for women?*

WEEK TWO

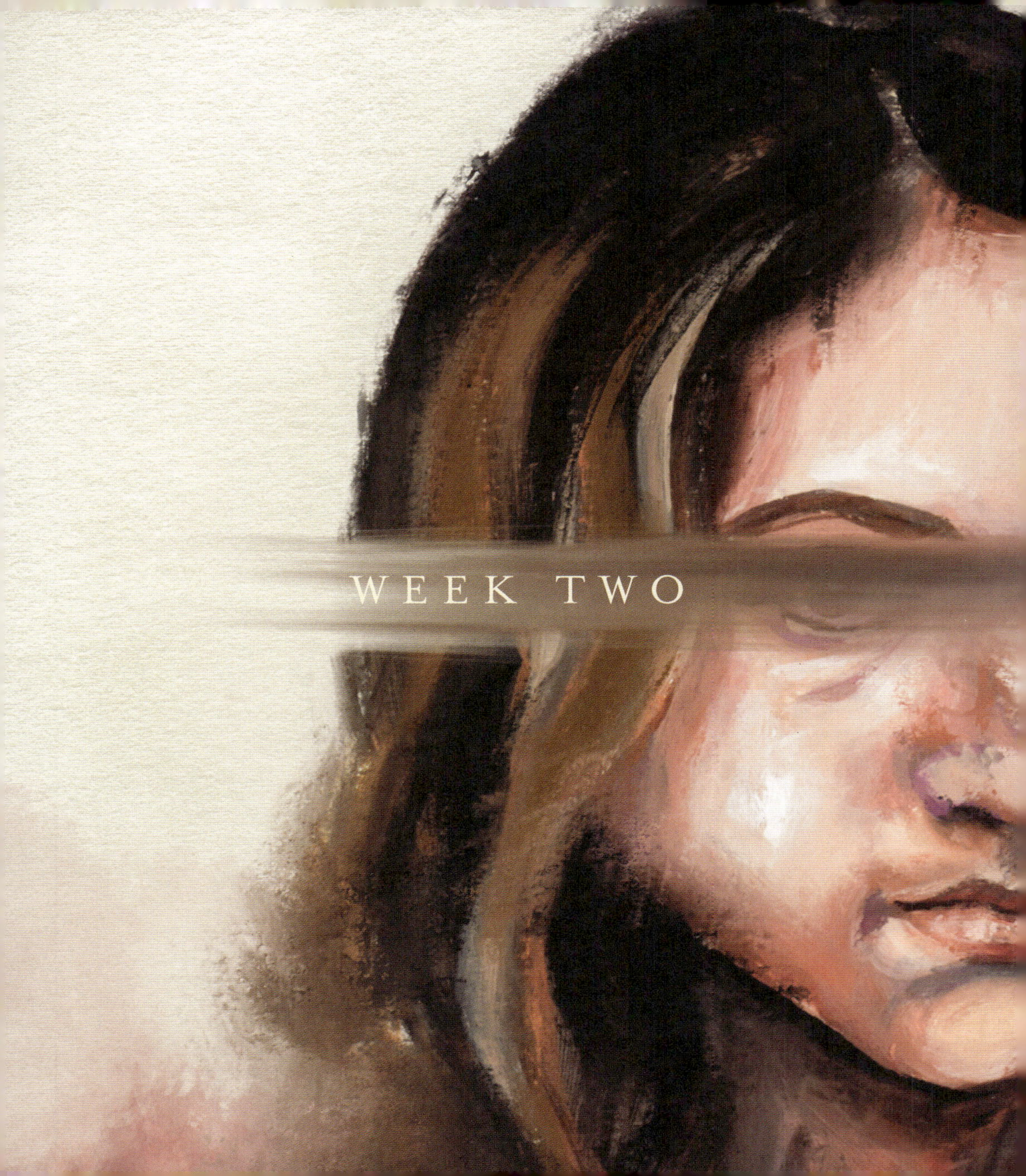

The

BROKEN

Self

Me, Myself,
AND I

What They

TELL YOU:

"I am just taking time to focus on me."

READ MATTHEW 22

What God

TELLS YOU:

"And one of them, a lawyer, asked him a question to test him. 'Teacher, which is the great commandment in the Law?' And he said to him, 'You shall love the Lord your God with all your heart and with all your soul and with all your mind. This is the great and first commandment. And a second is like it: You shall love your neighbor as yourself.'"

MATTHEW 22:35-39

A s a rabbi, Jesus had become quite the controversial figure. He did not neatly fit into the rabbinical schools' labels of his day. He perplexed the experts in the law because at times he seems to be what we might call very "liberal," and at other times he appears extremely "conservative." One moment, he is dining with a prostitute; the next moment, he is saying, "Be perfect, as your heavenly Father is perfect." These two extremes confused the religious leaders of the day, who usually fell on one side of the spectrum. And it likely confuses us too. We've been taught in our polarizing culture to always choose a team. But Jesus' life and teaching didn't fit into the stubborn theological categories his culture insisted on. So not only were they confused by him, but they despised him. And they wanted to trip him up and reveal him as an untrustworthy and inconsistent teacher. And so we read of many encounters between Jesus and the teachers of the law that record such instances. In Matthew 22, we have a bunch of these scenes in a row, introduced in verse 15 with a clue to the questioners' motives: "Then the Pharisees went and plotted how to entangle him in his words." The following chapter includes the Pharisees inquiring about political duties and the Sadducees' case against the resurrection.

Both conversations end the same way: the questioners end up stunned and stumped. But nevertheless, the Pharisees want to take another swing at it. And they come back to Jesus to ask one last doozy of a question, all in an effort to test him: "Teacher, which is the great commandment of the Law?" (Matthew 22:36). Will Jesus give them what they want to hear? Will he say something controversial and divisive? Will he trip up? The Pharisees have given up on quarreling over peripheral matters. This question goes right to the heart of Jesus' ministry: what did he think was the most important part of the Law of Moses? What did he think is the greatest duty of God's people? And while our attitude should not be one of arrogant scheming like that of the Pharisees, we should be just as eager to hear his response.

Jesus is as straightforward as he can be. The most important duty of mankind is to love God and love our neighbor. What Jesus would demonstrate with his own life and death, he would demand of his followers: life is all about loving God and loving others. This is the most basic instruction for human life. And one could even assume that since this is the greatest duty of the law, that it must also be the greatest defect of humanity. If God is most concerned that we learn to love him and love others, we must be naturally quite bad at it. And for most of history, people acknowledged that they were inadequate in the ways they cared for God and for others. There was a general consensus that the fundamental problem of human existence was the way in which we treat other beings. More specifically, it was generally accepted that pride was the most common problem for humanity. We were too concerned with ourselves. But the West today has brought about a new perspective in this timeless conversation. Generally, as we are told by celebrities and the media, our culture has come to the consensus that our problem is located in our lack of self-love—not lack of love of God or love of others. The voices that shape our culture make us believe that we do not prioritize our health and well-being enough, we do not make time for our emotional and spiritual health, and we are too busy loving others to truly love ourselves. We embrace an Oprah-inspired Christianity in which the gospel is more about loving ourselves than it is about loving others.

Unfortunately, this vision does not concur with the biblical description of fallen humanity nor the biblical emphasis on love. The Bible does not give us many tips on how to love ourselves. Why might that be? Maybe it is because the Bible is not all that concerned with our ability to love ourselves. Maybe it is because God is actually troubled by how natural and consuming self-concern is for us and how unnatural it is for us to be concerned about others. Maybe that is why the command is "Love your neighbor as yourself" and not "Love yourself as your neighbor." *It's because God assumes that you care about yourself, but he knows you often fail to care about your neighbor.* This verse is often read today through a "self-love hermeneutic," in which we impose our assumptions onto the text. It is not uncommon for people to interpret this command to mean that in order to love others, we must first love ourselves. But that interpretation forces the text to be about something that it isn't about. The command says that we need to learn how to love others the way we love ourselves and thereby *assumes that we love ourselves*. Jesus says that the duty of man is for him to love others just as much as he loves himself. Jesus is clear: the priority of life is to love God and to love others. We have just wiggled in our cultural sentiments when we try to make this text about self-love.

Some people who struggle with feeling positively about themselves might be offended at the idea that loving ourselves comes naturally, and understandably so. Many women cannot resonate with the statement that self-love is a default disposition for all human beings. Self-love may not be instinctive or normal for her at all. When she looks in the mirror, she is inclined to criticize what she sees, not to love it. Her life is marked by being too hard on herself and letting other people take advantage of her. She struggles with insecurity and lack of confidence in her personality, appearance, and skills. Certainly this woman does not naturally love herself! So has the Bible misdiagnosed the human problem? Did Jesus not realize that our real problem is an inability to love ourselves? Does Jesus wrongly assume that we love ourselves? I do not think so. It may just be that love as defined by our culture is not love as defined by the Bible. Culture often equates love with a feeling that affirms and celebrates the beloved. But the Bible associates love not just with a positive feeling, but also a will that works for the good of the other. *Love is primarily about concern for something.* It is a desire for the welfare of something. Love seeks out good for the beloved. It is, in this biblical sense, that we naturally love ourselves. We naturally want good for ourselves. And it is not necessarily a bad thing to want good for yourself. But Jesus' emphasis on love for our neighbor shows that our natural desire for our own good usually outweighs our natural desire for others' good, and that is a problem. We are naturally prone to care about ourselves more than others. We are naturally prone to focus on ourselves more than others. We are naturally prone to feel more pain when we are hurt than when our neighbor is hurt. We are naturally more inclined to feel joy when we succeed than when others succeed. All of this is related to the love of self. We care about ourselves. We want good for ourselves. And whether we *like* ourselves or not, we *care* about ourselves. In fact, it is because we care about ourselves so much that it hurts so bad when we don't like something about ourselves. If we did not have so much self-love (aka concern for ourselves), then we would not be so despondent over our flaws or insecurities. Loving and liking are two different biblical categories. The Bible does not claim you *naturally like yourself*. It claims you *naturally love yourself*. Whether you are confident or insecure, love of self is your illness. The Bible tells us so.

So how does Jesus' evaluation of the Law contribute to our reflection on the broken self? It reminds us that our focus should not always be on *getting love*, but rather on *giving love*. It tells us that the most important part of a godly life is caring about God and about others. It means that self-absorption is our sickness and self-forgetfulness is our cure. It means that "focusing more on me" won't ultimately help us. It means that "I'm learning to prioritize myself before I commit to other people" is sometimes a poor strategy. Our culture tends to make you think that what you have been doing wrong all these years is ignoring the importance of self-care. If you would just give yourself grace and stop letting other people control you, if you would just take time to pamper yourself, if you would just unconditionally celebrate and affirm yourself, then you would be freed from the grips of discontentment. But while it is not always wrong to give yourself grace, to treat yourself, or to be pleased with yourself, it is certainly not *the key* to a good life. Maybe if we paid more attention to the simple commands in the Bible, while trusting that God knows better than we do about human happiness and fulfillment, we would find ourselves feeling a lot more content.

REFLECTION **&** APPLICATION:

1. *Loving is the center of Christian living, not being loved. Can you think of ways that you make your faith all about being loved instead of giving love?*

2. *Love is the concern for something. You do not have to like something to love it. Name something or someone you love, but don't always like.*

3. *The broken self is dominated by concern for itself while neglecting its duty to be concerned with God and others. How much of your day do you spend thinking about yourself? How much of your day do you spend thinking of others? How much of your day do you spend thinking about God?*

Naked and

UNASHAMED

What They

TELL YOU:

"Never apologize for pursuing your happiness."

JEREMIAH 5:1 - 6:15

What God

TELLS YOU:

"'Were they ashamed when they committed abomination? No, they were not at all ashamed; they did not know how to blush. Therefore they shall fall among those who fall; at the time that I punish them, they shall be overthrown,' says the Lord."

JEREMIAH 6:15

The book of Jeremiah can be hard to swallow. Jeremiah spoke a message of destruction to his own people. He had the burdensome task of telling the people of Judah that God was about to punish their sins. The city was about to be taken down. It is a gruesome book. It is sometimes terrifying. It is exactly the kind of message that our therapeutic culture cannot bear to read. It's the kind of teaching that makes people today say, "I don't worship a God like that. I worship a God of love." But in humility and faith, we approach this passage as the very Word of God and wonder what insight it might have for us as we continue our study on our identity as sinners. Jeremiah 6 begins with the news that God is going to destroy his beloved city, Jerusalem. Jeremiah calls for the trumpets to be blown so that all may know and flee the coming destruction. He is desperate for his stubborn people to give heed to his serious warning. Jeremiah cannot water down this message. The reality is that "This is the city that *must be* punished; there is nothing but oppression within her"(Jeremiah 6:6). But even Jeremiah struggles to proclaim such depressing news. He grows weary preaching a message no one wants to hear: "Behold, the word of the LORD is to them an object of scorn; they take no pleasure in it" (Jeremiah 6:10).

The people of God run after injustice and their leaders support it by providing them with false confidence and security. They say, "'Peace, peace' when there is no peace" (Jeremiah 6:14). It is at this point Jeremiah bewails the lack of shame within his people. Notice that the absence of shame is related to their neglect of the severity of their sin. Their leaders encouraged them not to worry, saying "Peace!" By doing this, the leaders "healed the wound of my people lightly" (Jeremiah 6:14). They tried to lighten the load of sin by denying the seriousness of it and acting as if everything was okay. Poor Jeremiah was given the duty to tell them exactly what no one wants to hear: "No peace! Destruction is coming and it is your fault" (that's my translation of Jeremiah 6). Sinful religious leaders perpetuate the people's delusion of innocence and safety, but the faithful servant of God speaks the unwanted truth. Can you think of any voices chanting on social media, "Peace! Peace!" to you in your self-image problems? Do you hear their voices telling you to abandon shame and trade it for confidence? "You are enough. You are worthy. You are perfect just the way you are." They heal your sense of shame with affirmation and a declaration that you have nothing to worry about. Their words operate in the same deceptive ways as they did for the Israelites. They allow people to think of shame as an inappropriate evaluation of themselves at all times. The leaders of Israel in the 6th century BC did the same thing as the leaders of the American West in 2022: they want you to think that you are always in the right and have nothing to be ashamed of.

But in verse 15, God gives an opposing message. You can hear the sarcasm in Jeremiah's rhetoric. He wants us to see the stupidity in shame avoidance when we have sinned greatly. It's almost as if he is saying, "Was the serial killer ashamed of his mass murders? No, not even a bit. He did not even blush with embarrassment. He was proud." When we put it in those words, it is probably easier for us to agree with what Jeremiah is saying. We can agree that there is a time and place for shame. But our culture is going to reserve shame only for the very limited number of the cultural "no-no's" in our day. You should be ashamed if you don't associate with the correct political party. You should be ashamed if you don't affirm homosexuality. You should be ashamed if you appear intolerant in any way. But to be ashamed of loving yourself, never! To be ashamed of decisions you make sexually, never! To be ashamed of past mistakes, never! Never apologize for being who you are and for proudly celebrating who you are! You are a hero if you learn to love yourself. Today we are told that it is the opposite of shameful to love yourself; it is a mark of bravery and courage. These are the arbitrary lines our culture draws for where shame is appropriate and where shame is completely unacceptable.

But per usual, the Bible draws its own lines and makes its own standards. The Bible sees shame as the appropriate state of a sinner before a holy God. Remember our distinction between sin shame and victim shame. The people of Jerusalem in this case are not victims. They have not been treated without dignity. They have not been belittled. Rather, they are the oppressors. They are the guilty ones. The reason Jerusalem is about to be destroyed is because she would not blush at the consistent ways in which she offended God's holiness and broke his trust. Not only did she not feel guilty, she was even proud of some of her mischievous acts. Jeremiah 6 is begging the people of God to pay attention to their sin, but they just won't do it. They refuse to focus on the bad news. They want the feel-good sermons of the false prophets declaring peace. They want positive vibes only. But their false prophets would do them no good in the end. If only they would have listened to the word of punishment, then they could have come to terms with the option of repentance. Indeed, Paul realizes this as he preaches the gospel. He quotes the prophet Isaiah saying, "For this people's heart has grown dull, and with their ears they can barely hear, and their eyes they have closed; lest they should see with their eyes and hear with their ears and understand with their heart and turn, and I would heal them" (Acts 28:27). If only the people of God would actually listen to the reality of their shame, they could repent and be healed. *But no healing is found in a false sense of security.*

It is the tendency of the sinful self to repress our sense of sin-shame. While we may be prone to feel shame for slipping and falling in public or when a girl has a better butt than ours, we rarely ever feel ashamed at our selfishness, disobedience, and disregard of God's Word. It is a mark of sinful nature to make shameful acts an opportunity for pride and yet to let the trivial and unimportant situations cause shame. God's people rarely blush at their blatant rejection of God's commands, but they often shed tears over appearing inferior before others in trivial matters such as looks, wealth, and popularity. The broken self has a reversed sense of shame in which the eyes of people's approval are more

WEEK TWO | *Beauty Not Beheld*

significant than the eyes of God's approval. Therefore, our broken self is bent toward being unashamed of sin, while being embarrassed over a piece of food in our teeth. Our tendency is to downplay the sense of sin-shame we feel and boost ourselves through distractions and "positive self-talk." But what we call "positive self-talk," in a lot of cases, Jeremiah would call false teaching. May we beware of the ways in which self-love and affirmation culture teaches us to always look on the bright side, even when destruction is inevitably on the way. As a Christian, our goal should be to forget the shame caused by the trivial things of life and to confront the shame that is produced from rebelling against our most Loving God. May we accept that shame, repent of our rebellion, and be healed.

REFLECTION & APPLICATION:

1. *Our sinful self has the tendency to be unashamed of our sin but ashamed over trivial matters. Can you think of a time when you were unashamed but you should have been ashamed? Conversely, can you think of a time in which you were ashamed or embarrassed and you should not have been?*

2. *How can acknowledging the validity of our shame be helpful for our sense of self? How can it be healing?*

3. *In what circumstances can "positive self-talk" be harmful? What is the danger of fostering a false sense of security?*

Perfect

IMPERFECTIONS?

What They

TELL YOU:

"God doesn't want perfection; he loves you as you are."

READ MATTHEW 5

What God

TELLS YOU:

"You therefore must be perfect, as your heavenly Father is perfect."

MATTHEW 5:48

"Do not think that I have come to abolish the Law or the Prophets; I have not come to abolish them but to fulfill them. For truly, I say to you, until heaven and earth pass away, not an iota, not a dot, will pass from the Law until all is accomplished. Therefore whoever relaxes one of the least of these commandments and teaches others to do the same will be called least in the kingdom of heaven, but whoever does them and teaches them will be called great in the kingdom of heaven. For I tell you, unless your righteousness exceeds that of the scribes and Pharisees, you will never enter the kingdom of heaven."

MATTHEW 5:17-20

M atthew 5-7 is a collection of the sayings of Jesus that
Christians refer to as the "Sermon on the Mount." It
contains some of the most famous teachings of Jesus
on godliness and ethics. Earlier on in Matthew's account of this
sermon, Jesus makes a statement that seems to respond to certain
misconceptions about his ministry. We know that Jesus was making
quite the controversial impression on the public. He was certainly
drawing a lot of attention, choosing a bunch of nobody-fishermen
as disciples, forgiving the sins of society's rejects, and, best of all,
hanging out with prostitutes. We can see how he may have been
labeled as the radical, progressive rabbi. The Pharisees were not only
shocked, but also offended at Jesus' association with sinners. But this
is one of the most glorified attributes of Christ in the church. We
are proud to serve a Savior who came not for the healthy, but the
sick, not for the righteous, but the sinner (Mark 2:17). This aspect in
Jesus' life bolsters our modern distaste for super religious people who
act all "holier-than-thou" and are so judgmental towards people who
are different from them. Therefore, the fact that Jesus was a friend

of sinners fits quite nicely into our preferences today. While it is true that Jesus is the ultimate friend of sinners, there is a dangerous assumption Jesus wants to warn his people about when they see how radically merciful, kind, and gracious he is.

Apparently, some had concluded that Jesus did not care about the Law because of whom he associated himself with. They pegged him as an antinomian (someone who believes grace negates our need to care about rules and regulations, particularly God's Law). They assumed that Jesus' fellowship with sinners meant that he was lax about the Law of God. *They thought that Jesus hanging out with sinners was equivalent to Jesus affirming their sins.* In more familiar words, Jesus seemed to promote a religion that was "relationship over rules." It wasn't about keeping all these rules—that's what the legalistic Pharisees were all about! It was all about relationship! However, Jesus confronts this assumption straight up. He refuses to allow people to think that his care and mercy towards sinners means that he has a low view of obedience to the Law. He emphatically corrects this perception early on in the Sermon on the Mount, saying, "Do not think I have come to abolish the Law" (Matthew 5:17).

Jesus clarifies that rather than coming to do away with the Law, he has come to do it, to complete it (Matthew 5:17). This means that Jesus' mission had nothing to do with a neglect of the Law, it was actually all about accomplishing and satisfying the Law. Jesus came to live the life of obedience we never did. Far from disregarding the Law, Jesus is the only person who was fully faithful to the Law. To make his point clearer, he warns his disciples that anyone who tries to take even one little detail in the Law lightly will be held accountable for such a mistake. Then, as if he wants to add insult to injury, Jesus corrects the notion that he is more liberal than the Pharisees by claiming that all who want to enter the kingdom of God actually have to be *more* righteous than the Pharisees. If people were confused whether Jesus was lowering the bar, he just lifted that bar as high as it could go. Not only does righteousness matter, it matters so much that our righteousness has to surpass that of the most religiously devoted people we know. That is a hot take.

Throughout the rest of Matthew 5, Jesus continues to give a bunch of examples of how his followers are to be morally superior to the external façade of the Pharisees, and he ends that section with one final conclusion: "You therefore must be *perfect*, as your heavenly Father is perfect" (Matthew 5:48). Did Jesus just say we have to be *perfect*? I thought the gospel was all about God loving us as we are and embracing us with all our imperfections! The former is *true*; the gospel *is* all about God loving us as we are. The latter is *false*; the gospel is *not* all about embracing our imperfections. The connection between those two ideas is a slippery slope that Jesus wants to protect us from. What is Jesus doing here? Isn't he being exclusive and demanding?

It is common today to see perfection as oppressive. Perfection is the unrealistic standard set before young women in the media. Perfection is the shame-machine that makes us feel unworthy. Perfection is an unnecessary, heavy burden to carry. Focusing on perfection is

✓ world view

what makes us discontent. It is by coming to peace with and having confidence in our flaws and imperfections that we learn to truly love ourselves. Perfectionism becomes the enemy of a stable identity. This is the voice of culture, and yet it is also a popular voice in the church. We hear phrases like, "God doesn't want perfection from you, he just wants your heart." In this popular view, perfection has not only been displaced as the proper goal of Christian living, but it is even seen to be the enemy, standing in the way of our goal. *Perfection is thought to be an obstacle on our journey to becoming our true self.* "Stop trying to be perfect," they say, and "just be yourself." It may seem easy to fit this type of thinking into "gospel-logic" at first. The Bible teaches us that God loves sinners, not the supposedly perfect people like the Pharisees. After all, the gospel is this: that "while we were still sinners, Christ died for us" (Romans 5:8) and that we are now saved by grace, not by what we do (Ephesians 2:8-9). The Good News is that we do not have to meet a certain standard to be God's beloved children. These statements are some beautiful and biblical truths; however, they are not *exhaustive* truths and left alone could ignore so much of what it means to be a child of God. The gospel is not merely God's act of justification of sinners, but his *transformation* of sinners.

To say that Jesus loves us in our imperfections is wonderfully true, but to say he condones our imperfections is a gross lie. To say Jesus accepts us despite our imperfections is the gospel, but to say Jesus celebrates our imperfections is not. If God simply wanted to affirm our imperfect selves, he had no need to come down to earth to live a perfect life and die on a cross. He could have simply forgiven us and blessed us with no consequence and with no transformation. However, the true beauty of God's love is that he neither rejects us because of our imperfections nor does he let us remain in our imperfections.

The assumption that to love means to be content with the beloved's current state is a false assumption. To love a drug addict is not to leave them addicted and miserable. It is to fight for their health. It is to show them to a life better than the one they are stuck in. God desires that we reach our full potential and that means cleaning every spot and stain of sin. It might help us to understand that the term "perfect" in Hebrew and Greek is closely related to completeness. It refers to something that fulfills its purpose, that reaches its full potential. The Greek word translated "perfect" comes from the word *telos*, which refers to the ultimate end or destiny of an object. Therefore, to be perfect cannot, by definition, mean to resist our true self. Perfection is the true self. It is the goal, purpose, and ultimate aim of humanity. Perfection is reaching your full potential; therefore, it is not your enemy. The goal for which God created humanity was to be his image; therefore, perfection of the human being includes cleansing us from all unrighteousness and removing every blemish.

This all might sound better now, but still, what does Jesus mean that we "*have* to be perfect"? Does this mean we have to go to bed every night concerned that we lost our salvation that day because we weren't perfect? Thankfully, no, not at all. We can only make sense of this when we remember Jesus' former statement that he came to fulfill the Law. In other words, he came to be perfect. He came to fulfill the standard that we could not fulfill, and then afterwards to bear the punishment for our failure so that we could enjoy the benefits of his perfection. Therefore, through Jesus' life, death, and resurrection, *his* perfection becomes *our* perfection by faith. God did not lower the standard in the gospel of Jesus. He just carried us up to his perfect standard by the life and death of Jesus Christ.

The practical application for this connects back to the danger of subjectivism. When we insist on defining truth on our own terms, perfection can become whatever we want it to be. We can say some nonsense like, "We are perfectly imperfect!" We can choose to call good whatever it is we see in the mirror. We can choose to affirm everything we do. We can determine to be happy with ourselves no matter what. But this is not the way in which we break free from shame and discontentment. The self that demands that it be allowed to create its own ideals and set up its own standards must eventually surrender to the true ideal, the true standard. This means that devaluing perfection is not the logical result of the gospel. It is actually the opposite. The gospel of grace makes it possible for us to see and pursue perfection with hope of attaining it one day through the power of the Spirit. But the gospel of grace also warns us that a "righteousness that exceeds that of the scribes and Pharisees" will only be found in Christ (Matthew 5:20). In this way, the gospel both beckons us to strive for perfection while also reminding us that we are not saved by our perfection—not at all. We are saved completely by grace. This is the comforting message that Jesus was perfect despite our being imperfect. But it is also the hopeful message, that one day we will be made perfect as he is perfect. Let us therefore train our hearts to long for perfection. Let us salivate at any foretaste of glory. Let us delight to become who we were made to be.

REFLECTION **&** APPLICATION:

1.   *People often confuse God's mercy with affirmation. God loves sinners, but he does not affirm them. What is the difference between God loving sinners and affirming sinners?*

2.   *What is a healthy kind of "perfectionism" according to what we have reflected on today? What might be the difference between a biblical perfectionism and the biblically-condemned mindset of legalism?*

3.   *Perfection is not anti-gospel; it is the goal of the gospel. How do we keep a biblical balance between striving towards perfection through the power of the Spirit and resting in Christ's perfection as the only thing that will truly make us worthy of salvation? In other words, how do we balance trying to become more like Christ without thinking that we have to earn our salvation by works?*

ENSLAVED

What They

TELL YOU:

"You are free to be whoever you want to be."

READ JOHN 8:1-38

———

What God

TELLS YOU:

"Jesus answered them, 'Truly, truly, I say to you, everyone who practices sin is a slave to sin.'"

JOHN 8:34

In John 8, as Jesus teaches in the temple (making gutsy claims
about his identity and his connection to the Father), he stirs up a
lot of controversy. But despite the doubt of the Pharisees, many
of those at the temple took hold of the promises of Christ taught that
day and believed (John 8:30). Jesus responds to the faith of this group
of Jews with a call to true discipleship: if they want to prove their belief
is genuine, they need to abide in Jesus' word (John 8:31). His call to
abide in him is lost when the audience hears his final words: "and
you will know the truth, and the truth will set you free" (John 8:32).
They immediately push back saying, "We are offspring of Abraham
and have never been enslaved to anyone. How is it that you say, 'You
will become *free*?'" (John 8:33). If you read on, you will find this
dispute ends in their rejection of Jesus, even an attack on him. These
Jews were interested in the gospel as far as what it claimed about Jesus
(that he is from the Father), but were offended by the gospel insofar
as what it claimed about them (that they were inherently slaves). *Their
original belief in Christ is deconstructed by their insistence on maintaining a certain
identity.* They could not embrace who Jesus was if it meant embracing a

vision of themselves they did not like. Sound familiar? Certainly, we can begin to see a parallel to our current day.

How does Jesus respond to their question of identity? How are these people, the sons of Abraham, supposedly slaves? Not only were they not physically slaves to any worldly master, but they were not religious slaves either. They are God's chosen people. They are the nation that God blessed through Abraham's lineage. There was no sense in which these people were slaves! And if we were being told these words, we would likely have the same reaction. We are not slaves to anyone! But Jesus' offers a different category of slavery, one of which claims priority as far as our ultimate identity goes. They may not be slaves in other senses, but to Jesus, in the most important sense, they are an enslaved people.

So what is that sense? It is a theological slavery. Jesus claims that any one who practices sin is a slave to sin (John 8:34). In Jesus' understanding, if you are a sinner, then you are a slave. And when you trade obedience for disobedience, you also trade masters: the authority of God is traded for the grip of sin. This is the grand deception of sin: in the Garden, the serpent wanted Eve to think that by sinning she would become her own master, that she would no longer be dominated by a higher authority than herself. But that was a lie. Eve was *unable* to be her own master. Her nature was essentially dependent. Eve was unable to be completely free from mastery. It was impossible for Eve to attain "freedom," if we take freedom to mean being under absolutely no authority. Eve had two options: live under the authority of God or live under the authority of the devil. Her act of sin was essentially bowing to a yoke of slavery to the serpent. So it was for the Jews of Jesus' time, and so it is for us. Our sin enslaves us.

Still, we continue to believe the lie that sin is the way to freedom. We think that by getting to make our own decisions, unencumbered by God's rules and control, we are achieving ultimate freedom. However, we fail to realize that we are unable to be our own Master. It is impossible. The sinful state is merely the illusion that we are our own Master, so that the Devil can further tighten his grip on us as our true Master. We like to associate sin with free will. Sin is associated with our ability to choose for ourselves, and being able to choose for ourselves has widespread cultural appeal today. We love "the right to choose," when in reality, Jesus says the "choice" to sin is not the kind of choice we think it is. It is a choice tethered to a sinful nature that is determined to bring us to death. We might feel like we are living free when we choose to go against God's ways, but that feeling of freedom cannot last. If we're honest, most of us would admit that deep down, we feel caged in by *something*. Sadly, the way we try to fix that is by asserting our independence even more.

This delusion of independence fostering freedom is reinforced by the "psychologizing" of the self that is common in our culture today. We think of ourselves in predominantly psychological ways. Our psyche—our mind, thoughts, and feelings—is what defines who we are and what is good. How we think about ourselves and how we feel about ourselves is commonly seen as authoritative. And therefore, any person or institution (including God and the church) who tells us to be or do something our psyche doesn't like is to be overthrown. We see their standards as oppressive; and therefore, we see disregarding those standards as freedom. This is, at its root, the same act of Eve in the Garden. She didn't want another person to have a say over her identity, so she let her feelings define her, and she disregarded God's design. She found, however, that allowing her own thoughts to define her did not result in the freedom she was hoping for. In reality, she had just traded a loving Maker and Provider for a ruthless, deceptive Slaveholder. And therefore, "slave" is, sadly, an accurate identity label for all offspring of Eve, including you and me.

Contrary to popular belief, it is not by throwing off God's standards and expectations that you will find freedom. In reality, only the truth can set you free, and you do not decide the truth. If we continue to insist on being independent from God, we will never taste true freedom. Think of it this way: an object can only do what it is made to do when it functions in the correct environment. A train can only travel on its tracks. Only on the tracks is a train "free" to be what it was made to be. Off the tracks, the train is hopelessly stuck. Often, just like Eve, we are like a train stuck off its track, trying to convince ourselves that we are free to go wherever we please, when in actuality, we can't move a muscle. We refuse to hop on the tracks (God's design) because we don't want to let the tracks "define us." So we miss out on true freedom because we are too arrogant to recognize our need for the tracks. God's standards are the tracks for our train, and until we are willing to function the way we were made to, we will be living a life of false freedom.

If we want to take seriously Jesus' offer of freedom, we must first take seriously his claim that we are slaves. Only the person who recognizes their chains can break free from them. We must put ourselves in the shoes of the Jews who originally believed Jesus' teaching in the temple that day, but ultimately walked away offended. Will we let the devil convince us that a life of sin is freedom, and therefore, reject the authority of Jesus? Or will we admit that our life is dominated by a power greater than ourselves and reach out for the One who has a true claim on our bodies and souls? Will we insist on "being our own Master," denying that we are hopelessly stuck in the grip of sin everyday? Or will we come under a Good Master, a Master that longs to love us, redeem us, and glorify us, a Master that longs to set us free? Do not let your identity as a slave to sin make you walk away from the gospel. The gospel is its only remedy.

REFLECTION & APPLICATION:

1. *In what way are we slaves? Where can you see your "slavery" to sin in your life?*

2. *Why is sinful freedom a delusion? How do we attain true freedom?*

3. *Why is it important to understand our sinful identity as slaves?*

Blinded To

BEAUTY

What They

TELL YOU:

"You decide what's beautiful!"

READ MARK 14

What God

TELLS YOU:

*"But Jesus said, 'Leave her alone. Why do you trouble her?
She has done a beautiful thing to me.'"*

READ MARK 14:16

It is just days before Passover, and the religious leaders are scheming against Jesus while he is in Bethany. The time of his death is drawing near quickly. In fact, this is one of the last stories Mark provides us with before we begin the Passion narrative of Jesus' humiliation and death. Very soon, Jesus will be betrayed and put on trial. The death and resurrection he has tried to warn his disciples of will soon become a reality before their very eyes. But with yet another warning of his quickly approaching death, we are told a story that offers a sort of prophetic symbol of Jesus' burial. A woman comes before Jesus with a flask of expensive ointment and pours it upon his head. The bystanders' reaction provides us with a key insight concerning how our sinful nature often interprets beauty. With anger and a touch of arrogance they mumble, "Why was the ointment wasted like that? For this ointment could have been sold for more than three hundred denarii and given to the poor" (Mark 14:4). They even have the nerve to scold the woman. What might this text tell us about our identity as sinners and its connection to beauty?

Jesus quickly comes to the defense of the woman and his choice of words are poignant: "Leave her alone. Why do you trouble her? She has done a *beautiful* thing to me" (Mark 14:6). Jesus advocates for this woman's action on the basis of its beauty. They ought not rebuke her because she has done a *beautiful* thing. It may be helpful for us to understand that the Greek word translated "beautiful" in this verse is most commonly translated "good" in the New Testament. But when describing a physical object, translators opt for rendering this word more specifically than "good." We see this in Luke 21:5 as the disciples gaze at the temple "adorned with *noble* stones" and in the parable where Jesus speaks of "*fine* pearls" in Matthew 13:45. What scholars carefully notice in these texts is that the term "good" is not purely to describe actions that are right and wrong like we might think of it. The term "good" also describes physical forms like a stone or a pearl and so describes them as physical manifestations of the "good," the proper, the praiseworthy, the glorious, the excellent, and the honorable. The ability of a physical object to communicate goodness is its beauty; and therefore, scholars choose "beautiful" as the best translation of our text at hand. Not only was the woman's act of anointing a *good* act, it was a *beautiful* act. It was a physical manifestation of goodness. It was a powerful, physical portrait of truth. Strong's concordance puts it this way, the word "beautiful" describes the action "as an outward sign of the inward good, noble, honorable character." It is "good, worthy, honorable, noble, and *seen* to be so." And so beauty, in this case, is *goodness made visible.*

What does this passage teach us about our sinful selves when it comes to interpreting the world around us? It teaches us that since we have a distorted perception of the good, we necessarily also have a distorted perception of the beautiful. We are prone, like the people at the house in Bethany, to look upon certain situations and regard them as ugly (physically illuminating that which is wrong), rather than beautiful (physically illuminating that which is good). The people scolded the woman for her act because they did not understand the truth that it manifested to them. Because they thought her act represented something bad (wasting resources that could have been given to the poor), they regarded it as "ugly." But because Jesus saw that the act represented something good and true (his death), he regarded it as beautiful. Indeed, this was a beautiful act precisely because it was a visible portrayal of the gospel: that Christ would die for our sins. Jesus recognizes this saying, "She has done what she could; she has anointed my body beforehand for burial. And truly, I say to you, wherever the gospel is proclaimed in the whole world, what she has done will be told in memory of her" (Mark 14:8-9). This woman had just illustrated the Good News, but because the people were blinded to the goodness of that Good News, they were blinded to the beauty of her deed.

This is the fallen state of humanity without Christ. We are disposed to misinterpret beauty. We "see" as Eve "saw," not as God "saw." We fail to recognize how beauty and goodness are intimately connected. We want to make beauty just a matter of preference. We define beauty as anything that is appealing to us. If we do not *like* what we see, then it is not beautiful. If we do *like* what we see, then it is beautiful. But our concept of beauty is misguided in this way. We do not always realize that if something is beautiful, it is beautiful because it communicates goodness to us in some way that we may not even realize. Beauty itself is an expression, even a revelation, of goodness. It is a way of confronting us with God's goodness without words. It is an artistic confrontation with goodness—not an intellectual confronation. And this goodness is anything but a matter of preference. Because beauty is a manifestation of something we often distort (goodness), beauty is often not beheld. And arguably even worse, the ugly is rarely beheld. We rarely perceive the true nature of things in our world as ugly because we do not understand goodness. Later on, we will discuss the discernment it takes to appreciate that which is truly beautiful and that which is truly ugly, because in our broken world, the most beautiful physical forms are often mere masks for inward ugliness. For now, it will suffice to say that part of our sinful nature includes the degradation of beauty. We can see this in our culture today that is more likely to appreciate pornographic Instagram posts from the Kardashians as beautiful, than to gaze into the glory of the Sistine Chapel, a symphony from Haydn, or better yet, the cross.

The people that day did not embrace the gospel that Jesus was communicating to them. They failed to perceive the goodness of the gospel, and therefore, failed to see the beauty of the woman's burial anointing. Too often, we also fail to put on our "gospel lenses" when we view the world around us. Consequently, we miss out on beholding that which is most beautiful, even daring to call ugly that which is truly beautiful. This reminds us that our culture's idea that beauty is all about independence and personal evaluation is dangerously misleading. Culture thinks that telling you to decide what is beautiful for yourself will fix your insecurities and empower you to celebrate all of your "authentic self." In reality, we ought not trust our own eyes when seeing that which is beautiful, because our eyes often misinterpret that which is good. If beauty and goodness are so closely intertwined, a misunderstanding of the good will also come along with a misunderstanding of the beautiful. We need to accept that our perception is often defective as sinners. Instead of conforming reality to our evaluations, we ought to conform our evaluations to reality. You do not decide what is beautiful. You do not determine what is beautiful. You *discover* what is beautiful, and you discover it by first discovering what is good. Learn to see the good—that which God says is good—and you will begin seeing a world of beauty around you: a world that communicates and makes vivid to you all the goodness and glory of your Maker.

REFLECTION & APPLICATION:

1. *What is the connection between beauty and goodness/truth? Why does it matter so much?*

2. *Can you think of something that you may have considered ugly before that now, as you put on the lens of the gospel, you might see true beauty in? Think of the withered hand of an old woman, her wrinkles, and tired body. Our culture that is obsessed with youth finds her ugly. But wrinkles communicate the length of life and hard work and are therefore truly beautiful. Stretch marks bother so many women, but they are often a reminder of the physical process of child-bearing. And in that sense, stretch marks are undeniably beautiful. Think of your own examples.*

3. *Why is our sinful nature prone to misunderstand beauty? How do you see this in our culture, particularly on social media?*

UNSTABLE

What They

TELL YOU:

"The only way to defeat insecurity is to fully love yourself;
you are the only one who can judge yourself!"

READ 1 CORINTHIANS 3:1-4:5

What God

TELLS YOU:

"But with me it is a very small thing that I should be judged by
you or by any human court. In fact, I do not even judge myself.
For I am not aware of anything against myself, but I am not
thereby acquitted. It is the Lord who judges me."

1 CORINTHIANS 4:3-4

In the beginning of his letter to the Corinthians, Paul addresses the divisions that are wreaking havoc in Corinth. Some people are committed to Paul, others to Apollos, and others to Cephas. Paul himself took some serious criticism from the Corithian church; he even had his own apostleship questioned. In response to this controversy over leadership, Paul seeks to clarify how he views himself, and therefore, how they ought to view him, along with the other church leaders. The Corithians had the tendency to exalt certain leaders with whom they identified with. They based their allegiances upon their evaluation of different leaders. They fought over who was worthy of prestige and distinction, but Paul rejected this notion of evaluation because he believed something different about identity. The church leaders should not be regarded in terms of power or prominence, nor should their evaluation come from the people. Instead, their identity among the church should be that of servanthood and stewardship, a designation given from God (1 Corinthians 4:1). They are merely servants of their Master, which is Christ. They do not *own* the riches of the gospel, but are merely *stewards* of its grand mystery. This is how

Paul wants to be regarded by the church. They had manufactured a false identity for their preferred leaders as if they were the source of the gospel rather than Christ. And on top of that, they had adopted a false identity for themselves, thinking that they had the authority to say who is the commendable servant and who is not. Paul corrects this false designation and calls for a new and proper view of God's leaders and of ourselves.

In order to help the Corinthians properly evaluate identity, Paul offers an important insight into *the nature of evaluation* when it comes to the servant of God. Paul recognizes that there is indeed a requirement of stewards that they be "found faithful" (1 Corinthians 4:2), or in other words, that they be *evaluated* as having managed their Master's resources properly. It is clear that Paul does not want to do away with evaluation entirely; it has an important role. But how can Paul avoid never-ending identity crises when he is constantly being evaluated for how well he is performing? Certainly, he did not always steward the gospel the way he ought to! Do you ever feel this way? Do you feel like the pressure of constantly being evaluated leads to an insecure sense of self? Paul understands that. In order to guard us from continuous threats to our identity because of the evaluation of others, Paul gives us this ultimate insight about evaluation: *the authority of evaluation depends on the authority of the evaluator*. It is of little to no concern to Paul what kind of evaluation the Corinthians come up with about him, for the Corinthians are not his master (1 Corinthians 4:3). The judgment of others was not Paul's measure of success. Any human verdict is of little significance to the servant of God. His verdict comes from his Master,

WEEK TWO | *Beauty Not Beheld*

who is the only one who has the authority to judge whether or not he has been faithful. So Paul will not let the constant opinions and evaluations of other people be a source of insecurity for his identity as God's servant.

From what we covered so far, the mindset of Paul may not seem all that countercultural to us. Paul's approach to a stable sense of self teaches us to never let the judgments of others define us. This is a common sentiment in our day. Paul is speaking our language! Culture tells you to forget the opinions of others and just be happy with who you are. Our society champions tolerance and a "no shame" policy. We think society should be a completely judgment-free zone when it comes to how we identify and understand ourselves. We resent anybody who thinks they can tell us our worth or tell us how to live the right way. Being a good person means that we never impose our evaluation on other people. It's a "you do you" mentality today in America. And so, at first, we might easily concur with the apostle Paul, echoing his assertion that the Corinthians have no right to tell him who he is or how good he is at being who he is. Paul is right to block out the haters. The only way Paul will ever find satisfaction in himself and his work is if he forgets the opinions of nay-sayers and stays confident. A stable sense of self requires dismissing other people's opinions. While this is an important piece of the puzzle, this interpretation leaves out one essential sentence in our text.

Directly following Paul's claim that he is not concerned with other people's judgments on him, he expands on his claim saying, "In fact,

I do not even judge *myself*" (1 Corinthians 4:3). It is paramount that we understand what Paul is saying here. Our tendency today is to think of the word "judge" in exclusively negative terms. "Judging someone" means that you're looking down on them. But the judicial term to "judge" used in the Scriptures speaks broadly of any kind of evaluation, opinion, or conclusion about something or someone. The judgment of the judge may be that the accused is innocent; it is not always a judgment of guilt. Making judgments is not always an arrogant thing to do; often, it is just using your discernment. But if we apply this broader sense of the term "judge" to this quote from Paul, it means that not only does Paul not condemn himself, he also does not affirm himself. *He does not evaluate himself at all*. He does not give himself a verdict. He does not consider himself to have the authority to say whether he is guilty or innocent, good or bad. He even admits that "I am not aware of anything against myself, but I am not thereby acquitted"(1 Corinthians 4:4). What does that mean? It means that Paul doesn't see anything wrong with himself, but he realizes that *a clean conscience does not equal innocence*. Certainly some of the worst horrors of history have been done with a "clean conscience," without remorse or guilt. Therefore, to Paul, others' opinions do not matter in evaluating himself *and* his *own* opinion does not matter in evaluating himself. Neither party has the authority to evaluate. Only the Master has the authority to evaluate, and therefore, only the Master's evaluation matters.

Now you are starting to see how Paul is saying something quite different from our culture today. Paul is not saying, "Forget the standards people impose on you and create your own standards! Just celebrate who you are!" Paul is disregarding people's opinions. But Paul is not creating his own standards. He realizes that the only one who has the authority to ultimately evaluate him as a person is The Judge—God himself. The Lord is the one who will have the final say on who Paul is. Other people have no authority to declare Paul innocent nor guilty. And Paul himself has no authority to declare himself innocent nor guilty! Only the Lord is the True Judge. Paul warns the Corinthians not to make judgment before the judgment of God is declared. It is not from man that each of us will receive our "commendation" (or approval); it is from God (1 Corinthians 4:5). For Paul, he is waiting to hear the words "well done good and faithful servant" from his Master. He will not be satisfied with the praise of man, and he will not be satisfied with praising himself!

Most people today will agree that if you always seek the approval of others, you will end up feeling empty every time. The Bible confirms this to be true. However, culture's popular solution to this emptiness is self-approval. This is why we emphasize self-love, self-care, and self-confidence. We think that *we are the only trustworthy source of identity affirmation for ourselves*. We have to look inward to find peace with who we are and what we've done. But that is the opposite of what Paul suggests when he faces criticism and opposition to his identity as God's beloved servant. Paul does not look inward. He looks outward. By doing this, Paul realizes something we fail to. *The same instability caused by seeking the approval of other people is caused by seeking the approval of our own selves*. This is very important. Our evaluation of ourselves is just as turbulent as the world's, if not more turbulent. We long to like ourselves and be content with ourselves, but we are so often disappointed and embarrassed of ourselves. We fail to admit that the way we evaluate ourselves is just as flawed as the way other people do. If your identity-security depends on self-affirmation, then there will always be days when you are insecure. This is why people are so fragile today in their sense of self. It is because the evaluation of our identity is always up for grabs. Each day is another opportunity for failure. In his book, *The Freedom of Self-Forgetfulness*, Timothy Keller explains Paul's insight here with a powerful metaphor to explain how identity insecurity works:

> "[Paul] is saying that the problem with self-esteem—whether it is high or low—is that, every single day, we are in the courtroom. Every single day we are on trial...everything we do is providing evidence for the prosecution or evidence for the defense. Some days we feel we are winning the trial and other days we feel we are losing it."[1]

Self-evaluation cannot be the cure for poor self-esteem or identity confusion. We need a judge who has the authority to judge us; it is something we cannot do for ourselves. It is only in our reflection on the "redeemed self" next week that we can fully explore the redeemed people's verdict before the Only Authoritative Judge. But for now, beware of the insidious lies of our culture today. They are not a new

1   Timothy Keller, *The Freedom of Self-Forgetfulness: The Path to True Christian Joy* (LaGrange, KY: 10Publishing, 2021), 38.

device of Satan. Just as our enemy deceived God's people in ancient times concerning their identity, so today he often deceives us using the cultural trends that surround us. Self-love, at its best, can be a crutch for your ego; at its worst, it can be a vehicle for the work of the devil.

REFLECTION & APPLICATION:

1. Our sense of identity is haunted by constant evaluation. In what ways do you let other peoples' opinions of you dominate you? In what ways do you let your own opinion of yourself dominate you?

2. Our culture teaches us that the only evaluation that matters is our evaluation of ourselves. Why does this not work?

3. Who is the only Judge you can trust to evaluate you properly? How can you remind yourself of that daily and fight the temptations to let your own opinion be your judge?

WEEK THREE

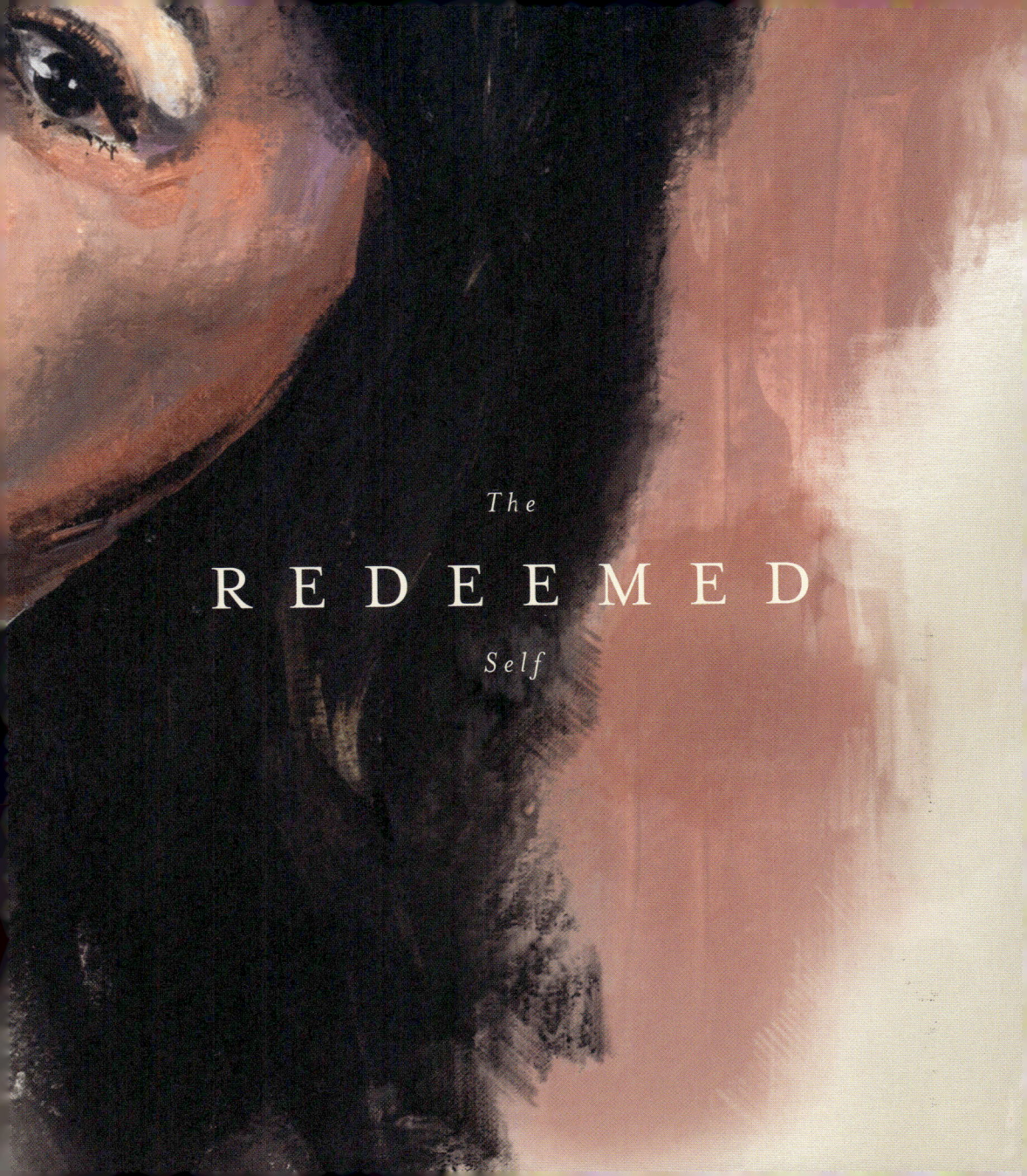

The

REDEEMED

Self

REDEEMED

What They

TELL YOU:

"You are worthy. You are enough."

READ ROMANS 3:9-31

What God

TELLS YOU:

"For all have sinned and fall short of the glory of God, and are justified by his grace as a gift, through the redemption that is in Christ Jesus, whom God put forward as a propitiation by his blood, to be received by faith."

ROMANS 3:23-25

As we try to understand the new identity we are given as believers in Christ, Paul's letter to the Romans seems like an appropriate starting place. It is Paul's most thorough explanation of the basic doctrines of the gospel. In the first three chapters of Romans, Paul labors to explain to the church how serious their sinful condition apart from Christ truly is. It comes to a climax of sorts in his poetic arrangement of quotes from the Psalms: "none is righteous, no not one; no one understands; no one seeks God," and so on and so forth (*see also Romans 3:10-18*). His conclusion from this realization of the severity and universal nature of sin is that no one will be justified by the law. Our deeds will not justify us before God; rather, the law only points out all the ways in which we have erred (Romans 3:20). Sadly, the law makes it abundantly clear how miserably we have failed in righteousness. The law, which is good in itself (1 Timothy 1:8, Romans 7:12), becomes a source of condemnation for the sinner. They are not worthy of approval. The law stands to prove that they have failed the test. They are unworthy. Paul labors over this point because it is a prerequisite to understanding the true gospel.

The church must first understand that justification cannot come from their worthiness because the law is proof that they are not worthy; they are not righteous. They need righteousness from a different source. This is the key shift from the message of condemnation to the message of the gospel: there *is* a new source of righteousness (Romans 3:21). There is a new way of "becoming worthy," since we are not worthy in and of ourselves. It is a righteousness that can be attained through faith in the Only Righteous One, the Only Worthy One, rather than through our own performance. But this Good News of justification is all based on this important truth: "for all have sinned and fall short of the glory of God" (Romans 3:23). Only with that recognition can the Romans truly and fully understand the gospel.

This language of "falling short" flies directly in the face of the self-love gospel. It means that we must recognize our *unworthiness* in order to receive salvation. But to count ourselves unworthy is an act that fosters low self-esteem, is it not? Most people would say that telling yourself that you fall short of God's standards reinforces the lies that tell you that you are not enough, and therefore, you are not loved. But Paul doesn't see it that way. For Paul, regarding ourselves as unworthy and insufficient is the healthy self-evaluation that brings us to recognize our need for a Savior. Without the recognition that we "fall short," we cannot recognize that we are "justified by his grace as a *gift*." Therefore, our acceptance of Christ's gift of righteousness is dependent on the acknowledgement that we are not enough. If we were enough, righteousness would not be a gift; it would be our due. If righteousness is connected with our worthiness, then it is something we deserve, not something we are mercifully given. The whole gospel depends on accepting this statement: "I am not worthy. I am not enough." It is probably because we think being loved is connected to being worthy that we make the mistake of thinking the gospel says we are enough. But being loved is not contingent upon being worthy in God's economy. We are not loved *because* we are enough; we are loved *despite* not being enough. We tend to insist on connecting God's love for us with something worthy about us, but the gospel insists on doing the opposite. That's the Good News: *you do not have to be worthy for God to love you.*

If biblical self-image cannot say "I am enough," what can it say? It can say: "I am redeemed." Let's continue through Paul's thought process in Romans 3. He asserts that we are unworthy of salvation, but that we receive it as a gift. How do we receive that gift? It is "through the redemption that comes through Christ Jesus, whom God put forward as a propitiation by his blood, to be received by faith" (Romans 3:24-25). The two keywords that will help us form the proper self-image for a believer are the words *redemption* and *propitiation.*

Redemption is a common biblical term that refers to our salvation, but what does it really mean? To redeem something is to reclaim something. The word "redemption" is often used as a legal term in the Old Testament referring to the act of freeing a slave from captivity. It also commonly refers to a close relative who has the duty to stand up for and secure the safety of an at-risk family member. Therefore, redemption can refer to the buying back of someone or something. It is closely related to the word ransom: redemption often refers to the price that is required to receive someone or something back. One of the primary features of redemption is that redemption involves payment. So, why is the word "redemption" important for the Christian's self-image? Because, redemption assumes that there was a price to get you to where you now stand. It assumes that you needed to be "bought back." Your salvation had a price. You needed a ransom. You needed your slavery bonds broken. To have an identity as "redeemed" means to understand that you needed someone to save you. It is an identity that assumes our insufficiency.

The term *propitiation* will help us understand how this redemption is paid for. Paul clarifies that redemption is accomplished by the propitiation of Christ's blood (Romans 3:25). Propitiation refers to the need to satisfy God's wrath. To "propitiate" God is to appease his righteous anger towards wickedness. Propitiation is the price redemption requires. God's justice must be satisfied. His anger must be pacified. We have sinned and fallen short, so we do not satisfy God's righteous standards. We need someone who *does* satisfy his standards and someone who can bear the guilt for our failure to satisfy his standards. What is the price for falling short of God's standards? Blood. "For the wages of sin is death" (Romans 6:23). This is a redemptive claim. There is a price to be paid to God for sin, and that price is death. How can that price be paid? Or, in other words, how can it be propitiated? By the blood of Christ—the only one who did not fall short and yet took the punishment of all those who did fall short.

Understanding propitiation is essential to understanding the gospel, especially considering the common distortion we find being taught in our culture. While we may not say it exactly this way, sometimes we end up believing and acting as if the gospel is the Good News that God lowered his standards and is now happy with us just the way we are. But that is simply not what the gospel teaches.

God did not lower the bar. God made a way to raise us up to the bar.

If we are offended at the idea that God has standards and requires punishment for those who do not meet those standards, we have forgotten to embrace our essential identity as being made in his image. Our nature and purpose is to reflect his glory and goodness, so when we distort the glory and goodness of the holy God, there ought to be a punishment. There are high standards because we were given such a privileged role. With much honor comes much responsibility.

The beauty of the gospel is *not* that God no longer cares about human beings properly imaging him. The beauty of the gospel is that Jesus is the image of the invisible God, the man with no sin, no stain; the man of 100% worthiness. It is only by identifying with him that we can stand confidently before God. This means that the Christian's identity is completely dependent on the life and death of Christ. We do not say that we are enough for God. We say that we have been redeemed. We have atonement. We are covered. All this dominates the way in which a Christian thinks about herself. She is not concerned with her own worthiness of salvation. She is enthralled by the worthiness of Christ and his love for her despite her unworthiness.

This is the identity of the redeemed: *made* worthy. *Made* enough. *Always* loved. And this love comes before the worthiness.

You are not loved because you are worthy. You have been made worthy because you are loved.

REFLECTION & APPLICATION:

1. *What is the difference between being loved and being worthy? Why is it an important difference?*

2. *Can you think of any spiritual disciplines that might help you remember your identity as redeemed? For example, keeping a gratitude journal can help us see ourselves as constantly receiving gifts from God. Rather than earning things, we receive them as a generous gift. By remaining in a constant posture of gratitude, we remind ourselves that even though we don't deserve God's blessing, he graciously pours it out on us.*

3. *When we struggle with believing that God loves us, what is a biblical form of self-talk to help us? Why is self-talk, such as "You are enough," not the most helpful or even potentially harmful?*

HOLY

What They

TELL YOU:

"Christianity isn't about rules, it's about relationship."

READ 1 PETER 1

What God

TELLS YOU:

"As obedient children, do not be conformed to the passions of your former ignorance, but as he who called you is holy, you also be holy in all your conduct, since it is written, 'You shall be holy, for I am holy.'"

1 PETER 1:14-16

P eter begins his letter to a group of exiled Christians with a reflection on the climactic nature of the gospel. It is the culmination of thousands and thousands of years of preparation. The salvation they have attained is that which the prophets of old longed to see and know. The long and winding path of the Old Testament finally reaches its destination and climax in the life, death, and resurrection of Jesus Christ. Many years ago, the prophets searched and carefully inquired, desperate to know the time and circumstances of God's great redemption. But the Spirit of God revealed to them that this glorious Good News was foretold not for their sake, but for the sake of those who would come to believe in Christ. The culmination of the kingdom has now been announced to these very exiles suffering in a land far off. They are the privileged recipients of the gospel message that angels long to look into (1 Peter 1:12). Peter wants them to understand the privileged role they have as recipients of the gospel. They may feel forgotten or like nobodies due to their current hardships in exile, but they have the honor to witness the beginning of God's kingdom on earth.

Verse 13 begins with "therefore." This means that Peter's following
words are the logical conclusion of his last statement. His declaration
in verses 10-12 that the people are the special recipients of the news
of Jesus has big implications. The words of verses 13-16 are the
imperative (a command) that flows out of Peter's former reflection,
namely that these people are the heirs of the gospel long awaited.
The command is that they prepare their minds for action, set their
hope on Jesus' return, and be holy. In Peter's mind, their identity
as the beneficiaries of the gospel transforms their daily lives. That's
why verse 13 is connected to verse 12 with "therefore." When they
recognize that they are the people to whom God has gifted the salvation
of Christ, it will turn their whole world upside down. Now, their lives
are to be dominated by the anticipation of Christ's return. Their lives
are to be defined by their expectation and confidence in the coming
salvation of Jesus. As recipients of the gospel, they receive the identity
of "obedient children" (1 Peter 1:14). It is this specific identity that is
the basis for daily holiness.

Peter knows that the gospel is "according to [God's] great mercy" and
is fully dependent on the "resurrection of Jesus Christ from the dead"
(1 Peter 1:3), but that doesn't stop him from seeing the gospel as a
call to holiness, as well. He knows salvation is a free gift from God,
but he also knows it comes with a commitment. We may be tempted
to think of attention to holiness as legalistic and a type of works-
based righteousness. Therefore, we may be inclined to view holiness
as anti-gospel. But Peter has the opposite inclination. The gospel of
free mercy in Jesus Christ is the *opportunity for* holiness, not the excuse

to neglect it. The gospel comes with an identity that calls us "obedient children." We are those who have come under the authority of our Father. We are *his*. And being "his" means we strive to be as he is. Being "his" means that our lives ought to be about transformation. The God who graciously called us into salvation now graciously calls us into holiness. The gospel identity as an obedient child now imposes upon us the call to righteous living. This identity as a child is intimately associated with a lifestyle or, as Peter calls it, a "conduct" (1 Peter 1:15). The type of conduct that is appropriate for the child of God is holiness.

This means that the gospel identity of "child" often has implications that we don't naturally associate with it. We tend to think of our identity as God's child as referring to our state of being loved by him and cared for by him. And this is indeed true, but there is also more to it. Peter uses the gospel identity of a child in this passage to refer to the nature of a child as one under authority. Obedience is the key mark of a child. Their identity as a child necessitates that they associate authority with their parents. So too, when we think of ourselves as children of God, we ought to understand that to mean that we are under obligation to obey God. This is the nature of being a child. The one who thinks of herself as a child of God not only thinks of herself in terms of God's love and provision for her, but also in terms of her *duty* and *obligation* to that loving God. In this sense, not all people are God's children. "Child of God" is a title reserved for the redeemed because, biblically speaking, being a child assumes that you are to be like your Father (cf. John 1:12). That is why when Jesus commands us to "be perfect" in the Sermon on the Mount, he backs up that statement with "as your heavenly Father is perfect" (Matthew 5:48). Identifying God as our Father insinuates that we ought to be like him. The child who truly embodies her identity is one who obeys her parents. She has a pervasive sense that she belongs to them, and therefore, she is under their loving authority. Living as a part of her parents' household, she is the one who conforms to their ways in order to confirm her identity as their child. And so it ought to be with us as children of God. We live out, reinforce, and celebrate our identity as God's children when we take seriously the call to obedience.

We can now see that the phrase "Christianity is about a relationship, not rules" creates a false dichotomy. Relationships and rules are not mutually exclusive; indeed they are intimately connected. Your mutually understood relationship with someone is the basis for the rules that guide how you interact with them. *Relationships define rules.* The unsaid rules for interaction with your friends are different than with your parents because you have a different relation to your friends than to your parents. This is how it is in all kinds of relationships. A teacher can enforce rules in the classroom, but not out on the streets. If you are going over the speed limit, only a police officer can hold you accountable. This is because you have a different relation to your teacher than to a police officer. Relationships inevitably create terms for mutual interaction.

Our relationship to God is no exception. Yes, of course Christianity is essentially about your relationship with God. But that relationship with God determines how you and God interact with one another. He now has a claim on you that he did not have before. Just like the Israelites, who received the basics of covenant-living with God (the Law) after being redeemed by God and brought out of slavery in Egypt, we too are given a new way of interacting with God after we are redeemed from our slavery to sin. Therefore, rules are not anti-gospel. In fact, Peter is giving believers rules to *reinforce* the gospel. According to Peter, these rules are an important way to apply the gospel.

We cannot let culture's categories keep us from seeing biblical teaching. Clearly, living in obedience is an essential part of our lives as children. In fact, obedience may be a spiritual discipline that can apply this gospel truth to our hearts. Obedience is the way in which we embody, and therefore experience, our identity as God's children. The fact that we *are* children of God is known and experienced in a new way when we begin to *act* like we are children of God. Maybe the key to embracing your identity as God's child is not always to "give yourself grace" or to remember that God loves you as you are (though sometimes that is certainly good and helpful). But maybe, overall, the key to embracing your identity as God's child means faithful obedience. Maybe it means the pursuit of holiness and a life that is set apart and devoted to the ways of God. Culture tells us that in order to embrace our true selves we need to express our independence and lay aside other peoples' standards. Peter tells us that in order to embrace our true selves we need to express our dependence and submit to God's standards. Obedience becomes a way to reinforce our God-given identity as children.

REFLECTION **&** APPLICATION:

1. *Does Peter think holiness is a requirement for salvation? No! How, in this passage, does Peter relate salvation to holiness? How are the two ideas connected in Peter's thinking?*

2. *According to Peter, what does it mean to be a child? How does one act like a child? How is this different than the way we usually understand being a child?*

3. *How can our daily obedience be a way of embracing our God-given identity? What is one specific area in your life where you could further embrace obedience to God's ways to help you embrace your identity in Christ?*

SLAVE

What They

TELL YOU:

"Never let people walk all over you. Never let someone control you."

READ ROMANS 6

What God

TELLS YOU:

"What then? Are we to sin because we are not under law but under grace? By no means! Do you not know that if you present yourselves to anyone as obedient slaves, you are slaves of the one whom you obey, either of sin, which leads to death, or of obedience, which leads to righteousness? But thanks be to God, that you who were once slaves of sin have become obedient from the heart to the standard of teaching to which you were committed, and, having been set free from sin, have become slaves of righteousness."

ROMANS 6:15-18

Romans 6 begins Paul's explanation of the Christian life. He has labored over the correct understanding of the gospel of grace, making it clear that we cannot be justified by our good deeds but only by the grace given through faith in Jesus Christ. Chapter 5 ends in that triumphant conclusion, proclaiming that just as we could be completely sure of our death "in Adam," so now we can be completely sure of our eternal life "in Christ" (Romans 5:17). Suddenly, the reality of our sin seems to fade away as we realize that "where sin increased, grace abounded all the more" (Romans 5:20). This is a key part of the Christian's identity as "redeemed." The shame of our sin that threatens the abandonment of God no longer looms over us, because of God's grace. We do not have to hide in the bushes like Adam and Eve because we can be completely confident in God's ability to forgive us in Jesus. However, Paul knows how easily this grand proclamation can be misapplied.

Immediately, chapter 6 begins with his anticipation of this mistake. He asks, "What shall we say then? Are we to continue in sin that grace may abound?" (Romans 6:1). He knows the mind of his audience. He knows that when he tells them that salvation is completely by the grace of God, they will quickly start believing that they can just live in sin happily because it will all be automatically forgiven and God's grace will "abound all the more." It is as if we end up thinking that salvation by grace is a warrant to continue in sin. But Paul is disgusted at the thought. "By no means!" he says (Romans 6:2). He then explains how faith in Christ is actually what *frees* us from the bondage of sin, not that which allows us to keep sinning without care. By faith in Christ, our identity becomes wrapped up in the identity of Christ. We "identify" with Jesus in his death and resurrection (Romans 6:3-4). And therefore, just as Christ died on the cross, so too did our "old self" die on the cross (Romans 6:6). And just as Christ rose triumphantly from the dead, so too we rise from the dead to "walk in newness of life" (Romans 6:4). This means we are no longer enslaved to sin. Sin no longer has dominion over us. Rather than being under law, we are under grace.

Then, as though he anticipates yet another misconception, Paul begins verses 15-18 by saying, "What then? Are we to sin because we are not under law but under grace?" He knows that when we hear that we are under grace and not under law, we might think that means we have no obligations. We might think that this freedom is an "anything goes" kind of freedom. Again, his emphatic answer does not change: "By no means!" (Romans 6:15). He explains it this way: "Do you not know that if you present yourselves to anyone as obedient slaves, you are slaves of the one whom you obey, either of sin, which leads to death, or of obedience, which leads to righteousness?" (Romans 6:16). In the first half of chapter 6, Paul addresses the fact that salvation by grace does not mean you can live happily in sin. You are free from the dominion of sin. But now, in the second half of the chapter, he takes it a step farther. Not only are you free from the dominion of sin, but you are to live under a new Master: someone else now has dominion over you. Lest the people of God think that this message of freedom from slavery to sin means that they are their own masters, that they can be their own authority, that they are not accountable to anyone or anything, Paul clarifies that we all have a master. And there are only two options for a master: God or the Devil (Romans 6:16). One Master demands obedience; the other master demands sin. Who will you obey?

What is most important to understand in this section of Romans is that Paul does not consider *utter* freedom an actual option for human beings, at least not in the sense that we think of freedom. Whether you sin or whether you obey, you are submitting to a master. And so now that we are no longer slaves to sin, we become slaves to something else: righteousness. In some sense, there is not an option for no slavery. It is either slavery to sin or slavery to righteousness. This might offend our contemporary ears and confuse what we have been taught about the gospel. Indeed, we remember the promise of freedom from Jesus himself: "and you will know the truth, and the truth will set you *free*"(John 8:32). Paul understands that, so he explains himself further saying, "I am speaking in human terms, because of your natural limitations. For just as you once presented your members as slaves to impurity and to lawlessness leading to more lawlessness, so now present your members as slaves to righteousness leading to sanctification" (Romans 6:19). Paul sees an analogy between the way in which we once offered ourselves to sin in our unbelief and the way in which we now offer ourselves to righteousness in our belief. Just as sin once compelled and constrained our life, now righteousness compels and constrains our life. Notice there is no option to be "uncompelled." We are all influenced by something, either by sin or by righteousness. Paul is not denying the freedom Jesus offered, he is clarifying its nature.

We must exercise caution here, lest we associate this "slavery" with the type of slavery we often think of when we hear the word. This is no slavery of discrimination, oppression, manipulation, or evil, like the slavery of America's early years. Paul clarifies the kind of slavery he has in mind. It is true that as slaves to sin, we were "free in regards to righteousness" (Romans 6:20). It had no claim on us. It did not control us. But, the result of the "freedom" from righteousness was death (Romans 6:21). So that kind of freedom cannot be that great of a bargain. But in our newfound servanthood under God, the result is sanctification and eternal life (Romans 6:22). Becoming "slaves" to God, when we think of it in this proper way, is actually becoming who we were meant to be. It is not oppressive and manipulative at all. It is the way in which we are sanctified, set apart as God's own children and conformed to his likeness. It is the process that culminates in the ultimate reward of eternal life, where there will be no more tears, war, or suffering. As it turns out, the servitude of the believer actually works for their ultimate freedom. Unlike our former master, our new Master does not compel us to manipulate and harm us. He is not motivated by power, he does not seek to oppress us. Rather, *he compels us for our good. He commands us to make us whole. He seeks to glorify us, not oppress us.* He is a Master that dearly loves his servants, even calls them his children. For Paul, this metaphor of slavery is just a way to put in vivid terms that as believers we are not "free" in the world's definition of the term. We are under the strong influence of our Master and his gospel. As Paul puts it in 2 Corinthians 5:14, "For Christ's love compels us, because we are convinced that one died for all" (NIV).

This idea of being "compelled" by another is unappealing to our culture. We live in a day where we are obsessed with our *"right* to choose." We have a view of personhood that sees obligation and duty as forms of oppression. Finding your authentic self is seen in terms of throwing off traditional expectations, religious expectations, or societal expectations. You are told that all of those obligations that claim to have authority over you are just forms of abusive domination. The creed of the modern self is: "no one gets to tell me who I should be and what I should do!" For Paul to speak of Christianity in terms of slavery is intuitively disgusting to the modern mind. Even if we clarify what this slavery means (that it is nothing like the slavery known in American history), the basic notion of being under another's authority is understood as people being coerced to be something they are not. In this way, our culture has adopted a neo-Marxist view of society and personhood without even realizing this. We view all relationships in terms of a power dynamic. We understand external forces upon us as a form of oppression. Just like Marx, we tend to think that we need to overthrow all authority in order to reach our full potential. But this notion is just simply unbiblical.

Paul has a vision of human flourishing that necessitates that we submit to authority. And therefore, the Christian cannot take on the identity of autonomy that is so common today. When we understand freedom as the ability to not listen to *anyone*, we have lost the biblical vision of personhood and actually exalted one of humanity's great flaws. This is not to say that all authority and power is good; certainly not. It is simply to say that there is The Authority and The Power that is good. To act as though "finding ourselves" means getting out of any obligation to that Authority is to ultimately live out a lie.

REFLECTION **&** APPLICATION:

1. *Do you ever use the gospel as an excuse to be comfortable in sin? How? What is Paul telling you in this passage?*

2. *Why does Paul use slavery as a metaphor for understanding our identity in Christ?*

3. *How can a slave be free? How does Paul understand Christian freedom if he is comparing Christian living to slavery?*

FREE

What They

TELL YOU:

*"Freedom means doing whatever you want whenever you want
and not worrying about what others think."*

READ GALATIANS 5

What God

TELLS YOU:

*"For freedom Christ has set us free; stand firm therefore, and do
not submit again to a yoke of slavery."*

GALATIANS 5:1

P aul's letter to the Galatians champions the doctrine of justification by faith. Paul labors, quite painfully, to get the Galatians to understand the role of the law in the Christian life and how one is actually justified. He claims that to undermine the doctrine of justification by faith by mixing it with a justification by works is to teach a false gospel. Throughout chapters 3-5, Paul uses the metaphors of a slave and a son to explain the essential difference between justification by works and and justification by faith. The "fullness of time"—the era of the triumph of faith—is much like the emancipation of a slave turned son. Once under bondage, he now becomes an heir to everything his father has. Under the law, we are held captive (Galatians 3:23). In Christ, we are released from captivity to the law, and therefore, are no longer slaves, but rather are sons (Galatians 3:25-26). Though God's people were indeed heirs to the promise of salvation originally given to Abraham, they were held under the guardian of the law until the fullness of time came in Christ. The gospel, then, becomes all about emancipation. We have already discussed that the term "to redeem" often refers to the buying back of slaves into freedom. It then makes sense that Paul chooses to use the language of redemption to describe salvation in this context. For those who were held in captivity under the curse of the law, Christ redeems them that they might leave their life as slaves and receive their adoption into sonship.

Paul's presentation of the gospel of freedom comes to a screeching halt as he laments the Galatian church saying, "But now that you have come to know God, or rather to be known by God, how can you turn back again to the weak and worthless elementary principles of the world, whose slaves you want to be once more?" (Galatians 4:9). Paul mourns in anguish over the fact that the Galatians have returned to the slavery of the law after being given sonship in Christ. Why would a son demote himself once again to the work of a slave? Paul goes down a rabbit trail in verses 12-20 as an expression of his frustration, wondering if his ministry to them has been in vain. He says that the Galatians are his little children for whom he is "in the anguish of childbirth until Christ is formed in you" to "until Christ is formed in [them]" (Galatians 4:19). After this emotional tangent, Paul returns to his thought of verse 9: Why would they return to the yoke of slavery? This is not who they were meant to be. By faith, they are the people of Abraham, heirs to the gospel of freedom. This leads us to our verse for today: "For freedom Christ has set us free" (Galatians 5:1).

This may seem like an odd sentence. If someone sets you free, isn't it obvious that they do it for your freedom? Paul seems to be stating something glaringly self-evident here. No duh, Jesus set us free so that we could be free. What is Paul doing here? Take note that freedom is a condition or way of life, whereas to be "set free" is an act of someone else that we received passively. "Freedom" is the present tense. "Set free" is a past tense. Paul is saying that Christ set you free (past tense) so that you could continually live into that freedom (present tense). He did not set you free so that you could keep living like a slave! Think of it this way: the Emancipation Proclamation of 1863 was the official, legal act that declared all slaves to be free. Did that mean that men and women who were held in slavery over the past decades suddenly began living lives equivalent to those of free people? No. In fact, we know from history that many slaves spent the rest of their lifetimes still living like slaves in a number of ways, despite the fact that they were legally free people.[1]

Paul is getting at something similar. Justification by faith is the declaration of our freedom. In the courtroom of God, we are declared innocent. However, in our everyday lives we often fail to let the practical implications of our official status as "free" to work itself out. We end up living into our old identity as slaves more often than we are living into our new identity as free men. This becomes more clear when Paul finishes his thought with "stand firm therefore, and do not submit again to a yoke of slavery" (Galatians 5:1). Essentially, Paul is saying, "You are free. You are justified. You are a child of God. Christ accomplished this for you so that you could live like it.

---

1   Of course, the reason they were not able to completely live as free people was not simply an act of refusal to live like free people. Many basic rights and freedoms were still denied them long after the Emancipation Proclamation.

So don't live under the slavery of sin as if you are slave. Stand firm in your identity as a child."

It will be helpful for us to consider this passage alongside Romans 6, which we studied yesterday. Is Paul contradicting himself? In Romans 6 he says that we are still slaves when we believe in Christ. We just shift from being a slave to sin to being a slave to righteousness. But in Galatians 5, Paul is angry that the Galatians are submitting to a yoke of slavery. They are not slaves, they are sons of God! So which passage is right? Is Paul losing it? That cannot be it. Rather, each passage offers a nuanced view of the Christian identity and addresses a different distortion of it. In Romans, Paul is addressing the misconception that the gospel of grace means we have no authority over us and have no obligations to live righteously. In Galatians, Paul is addressing the misconception that the gospel of grace is not enough to justify us so we have to do specific rituals and commands to earn God's love. Both are distortions and lean toward different extremes. You might tend to lean towards one of these extremes. You might tend to be very carefree when it comes to righteous living or you might tend to be arrogantly particular when it comes to righteous living. Either way, you are living out a distortion of Christian identity. What is important to understand is that the true gospel demands an identity that corrects both of those distortions. In one sense, we ought to view ourselves as servants of God, our Great Master, and therefore take obedience very seriously. And in another sense, we ought to view ourselves as free from the yoke and oppression of slavery, and therefore not be so concerned with rituals and regulations. Both passages are true. To prove the harmony of these two identities, Paul continues in his letter to give the same conclusion as he does in Romans! Christians should live righteously as a way to reinforce their God-given identity: "For you were called to freedom, brothers. Only do not use your freedom as an opportunity for the flesh, but through love serve one another" (Galatians 5:13).

The freedom we have as children of God is not the ability to do whatever we want (including sin), but is rather the ability to be who we were always supposed to be (through the power of the Spirit of God). It is the freedom to be images of God; mini-representations of his likeness on earth. This leads Paul into his conception of Christian living: we are under the Spirit, not under the law. Just as in Romans 6, there is not an option to be "under" nothing. We are either under the Spirit or under the law. Being free from the law does not mean that we can live however we want: "But I say, walk by the Spirit, and you will not gratify the desires of the flesh" (Galatians 5:16). And to walk by the Spirit means to live with "love, joy, peace, patience, kindness, goodness, faithfulness, gentleness, self-control" (Galatians 5:22-23). Yet again, Paul tells us the way to strengthen our Christian identity is to live righteously.

Jesus controversially taught his disciples that to sin was to be a slave to sin. He also said that to be free was to know the truth (John 8:32-34). Indeed, Paul echoes that sentiment as he reminds the Galatians that only the true gospel will set them free, not some man-made gospel. Both Christ and Paul have a vision of freedom much grander than the one we are fed through the media. Culture says that ultimate freedom is to do whatever you want and never let anyone impose their standards on you; the Bible says that ultimate freedom is the ability to devote ourselves to doing whatever God wants and to living under his standards. And so yet again, we find the identity of the redeemed cannot be primarily about autonomy and independence. That is not what "empowers" us. Empowerment, in worldly terms, is the freedom to sin. Empowerment, in gospel terms, is the freedom to not sin. And so it seems that we are tempted by essentially the same mistake as the church of the Galatians, but in a new way. We are tempted to buy a fake freedom. We are tempted to submit ourselves to a yoke of slavery again. For the Galatians, that meant focusing on the law and circumcision, having salvation become all about their good works. For us, it means pretending that absolute independence is empowering and having the gospel become all about our autonomy. Despite the different context, the mistake remains just as deadly. May we be warned that to trade the gospel of freedom for that of slavery is the most foolish exchange. Let us start living in the freedom for which Christ has set us free.

REFLECTION **&** APPLICATION:

1.   *How do we understand the statement "For freedom Christ has set us free"? What is the difference between being declared free and living like you are free?*

2.   *How does this passage make sense alongside Romans 6? In one passage, Paul says we are not slaves; in the other, he says we are slaves. How do both of these passages respond to a distortion in Christian identity? Which distortion is more natural for you personally? How does Paul say you can fight it?*

3.   *In what ways do you "submit again to a yoke of slavery" in your life? It is probably not by insisting on religious rites (such as circumcision) like it was for the Galatians, but are there other ways in which you allow yourself to be dominated by sin despite knowing the fact that Jesus has set you free from it?*

SECURE

What They

TELL YOU:

"Insecurities come from giving other people too much power.
Security and confidence come from inside yourself."

READ ROMANS 7:1-8:4

What God

TELLS YOU:

"There is therefore now no condemnation for those who are in
Christ Jesus."

ROMANS 8:1

We have already reflected on the unstable nature of an identity built upon self-evaluation. With the help of Timothy Keller, we used the metaphor of a courtroom: When we make ourselves our own judges, we put ourselves on trial day after day. Therefore, the verdict on our identity is never finally declared. It's always up for grabs. Each day, the trial drones on. Each day, new evidence is brought in—whether for us or against us. Some days we go to bed smiling because the evidence praises us. But far too many are the days we fall asleep ashamed because the evidence against us is stacked to the sky. As a result, our sense of self is akin to a roller coaster, racing up and crashing down, according to our performance. And because we insist on evaluating ourselves, we never reach the stability that we long for. We can never be completely pleased with ourselves, because the truth is, we are worthy of condemnation. We are worthy of a bad verdict. But on our good days we take the opportunity for a self-esteem boost and leave the courtroom foolishly confident. Nonetheless, there are always days we cannot deny the truth of the matter: we are worthy of judgment. We mess up. We fail. And so we consider the wisdom of the apostle Paul, who did not regard the evaluation of man nor the evaluation of himself to be the judge (1 Corinthians 4:3-4). His sense of self is dependent on a different Judge: God himself. Today, we carry on Keller's metaphor of the courtroom, but now we consider the courtroom trial for those who are in Christ.

If we turn back to Romans 7, we find Paul in the midst of an identity crisis. He is often doing what he does not want to do and not doing what he wants to do (Romans 7:19-20)! Can you relate? In one sense, his identity is one who is "of the flesh, sold under sin" (Romans 7:14) and yet, in another sense, in his inner being he "delight[s] in the law of God" (Romans 7:22). So, which is it? Who is Paul? Is he an enemy of God or a child of God? He concludes in desperation: "So I find it to be a law that when I want to do right, evil lies close at hand. For I delight in the law of God, in my inner being, but I see in my members another law waging war against the law of my mind and making me captive to the law of sin that dwells in my members. *Wretched man that I am! Who will deliver me* from this body of death?" (Romans 7:21-24). Paul needs someone to rescue him from this debilitating sense of war within himself. This leads to some of Paul's most beautiful and treasured words in all of church history found in Romans 8. One moment he bewails his confused sense of identity and cries out for help, and the next moment he triumphantly declares: "There is therefore now no condemnation for those who are in Christ Jesus" (Romans 8:1)! The "wretched man" he is in Romans 7:24 can all of a sudden rest easy. Why? What was the cure?

"There is therefore now no condemnation for those who are in Christ Jesus" (Romans 8:1). The Paul who could not decide whether he was a slave to sin or a delighter in the law of God now proclaims a final verdict over himself: no condemnation! He is good to go. He is free. He has been declared innocent. How? Certainly, we know that Paul is not completely innocent. He has told us himself. And was he not a former persecutor of the church of Christ? What does he mean there is no condemnation for him?! We find ourselves playing jury in the courtroom of Paul's trial and screaming, "Guilty! Guilty!" But Paul does not say, "There is therefore now no condemnation for sinners," he says there is no condemnation for those "in Christ Jesus." This is key. Paul recognizes that if his verdict were based upon his performance, he is in for big trouble. That is why he calls out for deliverance in Romans 7. His daily life is at best a conflicting mix of obedience and rebellion. But Paul is able to achieve security within his identity when he reminds himself of the gospel—the gospel that tells us that Christ went into the courtroom for us. He went on trial, literally—and an unfair one at that. He received the verdict of being guilty. He suffered the condemnation we deserved. He paid the price for our crimes. And now, we stand before the Judge to receive *his* verdict, Christ's verdict, not our own. Christ bears our verdict as guilty and we receive his verdict as innocent. This is the great exchange, friends.

We now see the courtroom metaphor come full circle. How can Paul find a stable sense of self when he knows that he is a sinner before a righteous Judge? Paul, through belief in Christ, stands clothed in Jesus' righteousness before the Judge. He passes the test. He is declared innocent on the basis of Christ's innocence. Paul can leave the courtroom. His trial is over. The ultimate verdict is in: *justified*. This is one of the most important words in all of Paul's writings. To "justify" is to prove innocent or to declare blameless. Justification is a verdict; therefore, it is the *final evaluation*. And Paul preaches the gospel of justification. And so you could even say that for Paul, *the gospel is centrally the message of a shift in God's evaluation of us*. Because in the gospel, you receive the verdict that Christ earned, irrespective of your actual performance. You go from being evaluated as guilty, to being evaluated as innocent. That is the gospel. God evaluates you according to a whole new set of evidence: the life and death of Christ. And therefore, Paul's justification is dependent on the righteousness of Christ, not his own righteousness. And now the courtroom session can be adjourned, he doesn't have to wait for a verdict. He does not have to wait for a judgment on who he is. He does not have to go into the courtroom every day to review new evidence. *All the evidence is in.* Christ has completed a life of perfect obedience and thus received his verdict, and therefore, so has Paul. The evaluation is completely secure because the work of Christ is finished. Paul's identity is not TBD. He will be found faithful because Christ *has* been found faithful. Because of unity with the perfect man of Jesus, "the righteous requirement of the law [is] fulfilled in us" (Romans 8:4)—"us" being those who, in actuality, fail to meet its standards.

What this passage teaches is that the key to identity security is actually to focus on Christ, not on ourselves. It is to focus on the declaration of the One True Judge, not try to make ourselves judge. If we refuse to let God be the judge and assert our own capability to judge and evaluate ourselves, our identity will always be up for grabs. Each day we could feel differently about ourselves. Even if we refuse to let other people shame us or condemn us, we will not be able to escape doing that to ourselves. We need to let God be God. We need to let God be Judge. Because of the great love with which he loved us, he has made a way to declare us innocent in the heavenly courtroom, and that verdict cannot be revoked. It is finished. This is how the Christian enjoys complete stability in their identity. Don't let self-love culture make you forfeit the security of Christian identity because it insists on making the self queen of everything.

Lay down your crown; you are not queen. You are not judge. God is. And thank goodness he is.

REFLECTION & APPLICATION:

1. *Disregarding other people's opinions can help give us a more stable sense of self. But it does not fix the problem completely. When we allow ourselves to be our own judge, how can that actually end up making us more insecure?*

2. *How did Paul find a secure identity out of the identity crisis of Romans 7? Does he look inward or does he look outward? Why is that important for us today?*

3. *What is God's evaluation of you in Christ? How can you reinforce that daily? How does that help you be secure in your sense of self?*

On
THE WAY

What They

TELL YOU:

"Don't try to change yourself. You are perfect the way you are."

READ PHILIPPIANS 2

What God

TELLS YOU:

"Therefore, my beloved, as you have always obeyed, so now, not only as in my presence but much more in my absence, work out your own salvation with fear and trembling, for it is God who works in you, both to will and to work for his good pleasure."

PHILIPPIANS 2:12–13

It can be easy to use the gospel of grace as an excuse for complacency. After all, yesterday we read the awesome news that, in Christ, we do not have to worry about our evaluation before God. We are officially justified; we are officially declared innocent. We have nothing to fear. The court case is closed. Therefore, it is tempting to make grace the comfortable, unthreatening place in which we live our carefree lives of sin. We no longer have to fear condemnation, because grace is the impenetrable wall that protects us from judgment and punishment. However, our sense of security can sometimes lead to complacency. When we feel smug and overconfident, we feel no urgent need to live a life of righteousness because our identity is set in stone and has nothing to do with our day-to-day performance. But to use justification by grace as an excuse for complacency is a grave mistake.

In Philippians, Paul addresses a church that is near and dear to his heart, apparently a congregation he spent much time with and intimately connected with. Paul takes joy in the Philippians' reception and application of the true gospel. He confidently declares in his greeting, "And I am sure of this, that he who began a good work in you will bring it to completion at the day of Jesus Christ" (Philippians 1:6). Do you understand the power of this truth? Paul is *sure* of their status in Christ Jesus; he is *sure* that they will finish this marathon in victory. This is the kind of certainty they can achieve when they find their identity in Christ. When looking at this verse alone, one might wonder if Paul and the Philippians believed the gospel was purely a one-time experience; that since they professed belief in Jesus, there was nothing else left to do. To assume this would be to isolate Paul's declaration and turn it into an excuse to live however we please. When we read all of Paul's words, we realize that our certainty and security in salvation is never an excuse for complacency. This is made completely clear to us when Paul commands the Philippians in chapter 2 saying, "Therefore, my beloved, as you have always obeyed, so now, not only as in my presence but much more in my absence, *work out your own salvation* with fear and trembling, for it is God who works in you, both to will and to work for his good pleasure" (Philippians 2:12-13). The congregation's initial embrace of the message of the gospel is not a one-and-done transaction. In fact, their original reception of the gospel is the basis for their continual application of it. Their profession of faith is just the beginning of a new way of life in which they continually submit themselves to the gospel. Not only do they receive their salvation (and are as confident in its completion as Paul is), but they "work out" their salvation daily in "fear and trembling"— not in complacency.

So, why does Paul not see the gospel of grace as an excuse for laziness and a negligence for repentance? After all, he is the one who is so confident that God will forgive us! The answer is that salvation is not *only* about justification (though it is never less than justification). Salvation is also about sanctification—unifying ourselves with Christ and being renewed by the Holy Spirit.[2] Therefore, the last thing we will do when we truly hear and understand the gospel is become complacent. The grace of God enables us to be filled with the Holy Spirit who is the ultimate transformer. The Philppians were commanded to work out their salvation with fear and trembling because it is *God*, the Maker of the Universe, who is within them when they receive Christ in faith. Paul flips our notion of grace completely upside down. For us, grace is the reason we *don't* have to be concerned about sinning. For Paul, grace is the reason we *do* have to be concerned about sinning. For us, grace is the reason we *do not* have to fear and tremble. For Paul, grace is the reason we *should* fear and tremble. *Grace is the power to become who we were made to be. Not the excuse to stay as we are.* Grace is not just God's forgiveness of our sins, but it is his dwelling within us. Therefore, grace is necessarily about sanctification because any place where the Spirit of God dwells is to be made holy for his stay. The thought of God's Spirit at work within us ought to make us shake. Not in fear of danger, but in realization of the glory moving within our hearts. We tremble at the potential beauty, not at the potential punishment. For Paul, the logical result of receiving salvation is working out that salvation.

2   In its most basic form, salvation includes justification, sanctification, and glorification.

We must also hear this command in light of the former declaration in chapter 1 about his utter confidence in the Philippian believers' final triumph. Paul is completely sure that God will be faithful and finish off the good work he began in the believers at Philippi. Nonetheless, in the midst of Paul's certainty of God's power and faithfulness, he also sees a necessity that the Philippians pursue and apply the salvation that is sure to come to them. Therefore, the certainty and safety of the gift of salvation does not insinuate that we don't strive towards it. Our knowledge that we will get the gift does not stop us from running towards it. The certainty of our salvation, therefore, is not an excuse for complacency, but the basis for change.

What does this mean for the Christian's redeemed identity? It reminds us that we are not quite yet who we ought to be. We are not a finished project; there is still much work to be done before we are rid of all our flaws. The Christian identity is aware of the tension of the "already-but-not-yet." In other words, there is an important part of our identity that is already realized: we are justified before God and that is done and secure. But there is another part of our identity that has yet to be realized: we do not yet perfectly image God as we were made to. In some sense, the Christian's awareness of self is unchanging and stable, but in another sense, it is a work in progress. This is how Christianity allows our sense of self to foster both contentment and hunger for improvement. The "already-but-not-yet" identity of a Christian fosters both the safety of guaranteed victory and the incentive for growth.

The "already" part of Christian identity can be satisfied in the sense that it does not have to fear abandonment or condemnation. You are *already* justified. No worries there. But the "not-yet" part of the Christian identity is an everyday battle. We are *not yet* perfect. Therefore, the "not-yet" part of Christian identity never stops striving for complete holiness, never stops seeking to be more like Christ, and never stops longing to be restored to perfection. We do so in full confidence that, though we may fail, we will ultimately triumph as grace abounds. This solves the dilemma between being content in our identity while also desiring to improve ourselves. The two (contentment and improvement) do not have to work against each other. Being content means that we can rest in the security of being in Christ while still striving to be the best we can be. Identity security does not have to mean compromising our high standards for ourselves.

We can see how this confusion between contentment and complacency manifests itself in our culture today. We often believe to be content means you must love everything about yourself. This is why we think that affirmation is the key to a secure identity. You have to shower yourself with positive self-talk and praise in order to be content with who you are. On the contrary, sometimes we are *too* focused on self-improvement. This is why self-help books are so popular. Indeed, even in the media, it is very trendy for people to talk about the ways they are trying to be the best version of themselves. They want to "be better" for themselves and for others. We especially see this trend in one's public confession when the media reveals some mistake or wrongdoing. Lest they be "canceled," they must go online and publicly acknowledge their downfall and explain what they are doing to "be better."

It seems as though here in America, we simply cannot figure out which way we want it: do we want to affirm everyone all the time or do we want to demand that people do better? We condemn perfectionism and are champions of "giving ourselves grace,"[3] but also want to push people to "be the best version of themselves." So, we say, "Be happy with who you are!" while also saying, "Be better!" Maintaining both views is hard. Affirmation culture recognizes that we long to have a secure sense of self that does not have to fear being insufficient or unworthy, but self-improvement culture says that we are also unwilling to give up all of our standards. How in the world can we resist perfectionism without compromising our standards? This is the question the western world seems to have trouble figuring out. Luckily—or better yet, providentially—the gospel is the answer to this tension. The Bible does not say that because we fall short of the world's standards, we now must live in a constant state of shame and insecurity. The gospel gives us confidence in our status before God, which is why Paul says in Philippians 1 that he is sure that God will finish what he started. The gospel not only makes a way for us to be safe and loved despite our flaws; it makes a way for us to never celebrate nor conquer our flaws. The gospel motivates and empowers us to choose a better way, and that

3   This is not to say that we ought not extend grace to others and indeed be gracious with ourselves, but we ought to take care that we are not "giving ourselves grace" at the expense of a personal pursuit of holiness.

is why Paul commands the Philippians to "work out their salvation," even though their salvation is safe in God's hands. The identity that rests upon Christ does not have to doubt God's love in the face of failure, but it also does not exalt failure.

Gospel identity solves the tension that our culture cannot seem to solve. It maintains a stable sense of self while also maintaining the perfect standards of God. It maintains the proper goal of perfection without leaving us in constant shame and fear. Gospel identity gives us stability in our identity while also calling us to transformation. All of this is accomplished through the person and work of Christ. So, fellow Christian, understand yourself in the glory of "already-but-not-yet." Both of these statements apply to you: "I am sure of this, that he who began a good work in you will bring it to completion at the day of Jesus Christ" (Philippians 1:6), and "work out your own salvation with fear and trembling, for it is God who works in you, both to will and to work for his good pleasure" (Philippians 2:12-13). In one sense, the Christian identity has arrived; yet in another, it is still on its way.

REFLECTION & APPLICATION:

1.   What is the "already" portion of your identity in Christ? What is the "not-yet" portion?

2.   Does our certainty in God's forgiveness and our salvation stop us from wanting to improve? Why is that?

3.   How does knowing that "he who began a good work in you will bring it to completion at the day of Jesus Christ" give us hope as we struggle day to day in "working out our salvation"? In what areas of your life do you need to remind yourself of the certainty of your salvation? In what areas of your life do you need to remind yourself to "work out" that salvation?

WEEK FOUR

The

PHYSICAL

Self

Why Doesn't the Bible Tell Me I'm Pretty?
A NEW TAKE ON PSALM 139

What They

TELL YOU:

"You are beautiful."

READ PSALM 139

What God

TELLS YOU:

"I praise you, for I am fearfully and wonderfully made.
Wonderful are your works; my soul knows it very well."

PSALM 139:14

The typical "body positive" verse that Christians will quote when discussing body image comes from Psalm 139. The declaration that we are fearfully and wonderfully made ought to be an encouragement to those who hate what they see in the mirror. That is a good thing, but our usage of it may sometimes result in an unbalanced interpretation that ignores what the rest of the psalm is really about. When we look at the entirety of the psalm, we find that David is more concerned with the grandeur of God and the pervading sense of his presence and power in our world rather than the beauty and loveliness of the human body. While this psalm does have a comforting word for the young woman who is insecure in her own skin, it is not necessarily *all* about her beauty; it is much more so about her God. This reminds us of the importance of context as we read and apply the Scriptures. When we investigate the total content of the psalm, we become convinced that to use this psalm for a body confidence anthem is not the wisest move. Sadly, we sometimes impose what we *want* the Bible to say upon this verse. Surely, this verse proclaims the dignity of humanity and the value of their physical nature, but when we insist on making this verse primarily about body confidence, we miss the point of the psalm by importing some meaning into the verse that is not there in the text itself.

David begins the psalm with a meditation on the Lord's omniscience and omnipresence. The Lord knows David intimately and is acquainted with all of his ways, no matter where he goes, no matter when he goes (Psalm 139:1-5). God's foreknowledge even knows David's words before they fall from his tongue. Not only does God know about David, but he is near to David. David can sense the presence of God all around him. David's God closely protects and guides him. His presence is pervasive in David's world. Therefore, God is both transcendent (far above and beyond David) and imminent (surrounding him closely). This reflection is too "wonderful" for David to comprehend (Psalm 139:6). The greatness of God combined with his nearness fills David with awe. He cannot fully grasp it; he cannot "attain" it. He cannot fathom a God that is so infinite and knowledgeable, yet so close and relational. As David ponders the thought of a God so awesome and near, he begins to realize that this God is also pervasive and inescapable. He cannot flee from the presence of his God. No matter where he goes, even into the depths of Sheol, God's presence follows him (Psalm 139:8). Even when it seems too dark to be seen, David is filled with a sense of God's heavenly eyes upon him (Psalm 139:12). Verse 13 explains the theology behind David's revelation of God's perfect knowledge of him: God is his Creator. He formed David. He artfully crafted a lump of cells into mini-David while he was yet in his mother's womb. This reflection of God's nature and role as Creator climaxes in the words of worship in verse 14.

When we read the psalm in its entirety, tracking with its overall content and progression, Psalm 139:14 is clearly an expression of adoration to God for his greatness as Creator and his close intimacy with us. It is a combination that blows David away. But when we read Psalm 139:14 through the lens of body-confidence, we lose sight of the very first proclamation in the verse: worship of God. David says "I praise *you*." He does not take delight in himself; he takes delight in God. As the context has shown, the thought of verse 14 is the result, even the climax, of contemplation on who *God* is, not who *David* is. The Psalm is about God. It's not really about David. David is merely using himself as an example in his meditation on God's grand creativity and care for his creation. The words are the result of awe, not self-confidence. That is an important distinction. Awe is humble amazement and reverent wonder in the work of one greater than oneself. Self-confidence is an assurance and belief in myself as capable and lovable. David wants us to feel awe, not necessarily to feel confidence. David's statement is ultimately rooted in humility, an understanding of his smallness before the great God who made him. He is bewildered by the fact that the awesome God of the universe is also his maker and loving sustainer which generates a sense of gratitude and astonishment within him.

While David's words in verse 14 come from a place of humility, our slightly flawed interpretation of this text is ultimately rooted in pride—an attempt to make something or someone exalt us when the psalm was written to exalt God. David's statement is a celebration of Yahweh. He is flabbergasted by the wonder of his God. And that fact is a humbling one, not necessarily an "empowering" one (at least not what we think of today as "empowering"). If empowerment is the self-perception of being independent and worthy, this is not David's self-perception. In his final words, you can clearly detect that David is not experiencing a self-esteem boost, but rather *awe* in this psalm: "Search me, O God, and know my heart! Try me and know my thoughts! And see if there be any grievous way in me, and lead me in the way everlasting!" (Psalm 139:23-24). David's realization of God's intimate knowledge and guidance leads him to beg God to make him *holier*, not to be confident that he has it all together. He is pleading that God would search him and reveal to him any way in which he errs. This is not the plea of someone who is self-assured and confident. This is the word of someone who is shaken by the undeserved provision of his Creator and who longs to be worthy of it.

We understand what Psalm 139 is saying positively about God, but is it not also saying something positive about humanity? Indeed. David's choice of words is intriguing: he says he is "fearfully and wonderfully made." Clearly, these terms are used positively. But what does it actually mean that David is made *fearfully*? Throughout the Psalms, "fearful" things (literally) are often translated as "awesome" things. The same exact word construction of "fearfully made" in Psalm 139:14 is found in Psalm 65:5 but is translated as "awesome deeds." The great deeds of Psalm 65:5 are performed awesomely, just as David is being made awesomely, as he declares in Psalm 139. The term describes an object or action that causes astonishment or awe, even fear. It is used in these texts as an adverb to express *how* something is done. By saying he was made *fearfully* is to say he was made in such a way that inspires amazement. It might even inspire terror. It might frighten us. It is so awesome that it is a little scary.

The two adverbs used in Psalm 139—fearfully and wonderfully— essentially mean the same thing: The way in which God created David evokes reverent worship within him. God's act of creating is so bewildering and terribly astonishing that it can make you tremble. It is so breath-taking it is almost frightening. This is David's realization of the deliberate, yet delicate divine involvement and intentionality in God's creation of mankind. David, though a speck in the universe, was tactfully and attentively formed. He is the handiwork of a brilliant artist who crafts all his works in "fear," in awesomeness, in utter power, in holy purpose, and in pure glory. Therefore, David's physical existence is a proclamation of the Artist's praise. As a result, David recognizes physical existence as something objectively beautiful. However, this does not mean he is flawless or *perfectly* beautiful. The Scriptures[1] make it clear that sin has corrupted the physical forms of this world. We are no longer 100% beautiful. Every human is a mixture of beauty and ugliness due to the fall. This may be why David does not say "I am beautiful" in this verse. Rather, he says something about the nature of his creation as a custom-crafted, carefully molded,

---

1   Genesis 3:17-19, Romans 8:20-22, 1 Corinthians 15:42-55, 2 Corinthians 4:16

tenderly woven, piece of art in the hands of his divine designer. He chooses the words "fearfully and wonderfully" because those words are consistent with the overall tone and content of the psalm. His reflection on a majestic God who is so near to tiny human beings causes his fear and wonder. While we may be desperate to read the words "You are beautiful" declared in the Scriptures, instead we find "You are fearfully and wonderfully made." Do you see the difference? One is purely a statement about the self. Another is a statement about our Creator. Surely, this verse is still an affirmation of creation and the human body, but it is rooted in an affirmation of the Creator. You will notice the passage has nothing to do with being "pretty." David is not saying he is a handsome, young man in this psalm. He is not affirming himself as attractive. The attention is on the way in which David came to be, not the physical appearance David currently has. It is more of a reflection on *how* God made David not necessarily *what* David looks like. And so if we are looking to hear that we are pretty, Psalm 139 is not necessarily the place to go.

Instead, we need a more robust biblical theology of beauty—one that accounts for the corruption of God's originally good physical creation. One that accounts for what beauty is ultimately all about. Have you ever heard a phrase along the lines of this: "When you insult your appearance, you insult the artwork of God"? This is the kind of phrase that does not have a thorough understanding of biblical beauty. *The Bible does not say that because God created you, everything about you is beautiful.* That would only be the case if the Bible stopped at Genesis 2. But Genesis 3 is our reality. You are no longer a perfect, unmarred image of God, whether physically or spiritually. Your body was created by God, but it was corrupted by the fall. Therefore, recognizing God as Creator does not necessarily mean that you have to love every part of your appearance. We acknowledge that there are many ugly things in this world due to the fall. Why are we so insistent that none of those ugly things show up in our physical appearance? The Bible may not say that you're pretty, but that really doesn't matter that much—and it wouldn't be 100% true anyway. If physical beauty is indeed dependent on someone's or something's ability to communicate God's glory, then certainly we must concede that not *everything* about us is beautiful. Your pimple does not reflect the glory of God, and that is okay. That is why Psalm 139 is a reflection on how awe-inspiring God's creative power is—not about how good-looking we are.

REFLECTION **&** APPLICATION:

1. *Overall, what is the message of Psalm 139? What is its main point? How does this help us understand verse 14?*

2. *Do you use your physical body as a way to be amazed by God's power to create and sustain or do you use your physical body as a way to exalt and shame yourself?*

3. *Why doesn't the Bible tell you you're pretty?*

You Are Not

YOUR OWN

TELL YOU:

"My body, my choice."

READ 1 CORINTHIANS 6

What God

TELLS YOU:

"Or do you not know that your body is a temple of the Holy Spirit within you, whom you have from God? You are not your own, for you were bought with a price. So glorify God in your body."

1 CORINTHIANS 6:19-20

T hroughout his first letter to the Corinthians, Paul addresses a myriad of moral issues ravaging the church. Most of these debates surround the question of Christian liberty. The Corinthians are arguing over what it means to be "free" in Christ. Throughout the book, Paul is interacting with multiple claims that the Corinthians have made through a past letter to him. The English Standard Version (ESV) indicates this interpretation through the usage of quotations as if Paul is referring to something they have said to him before: "'*All things are lawful for me*,' but not all things are helpful. '*All things are lawful for me*,' but I will not be dominated by anything" (1 Corinthians 6:12). The italics within quotations are interpreted as quotes from the Corinthian church to Paul with Paul's responses following. What we find in these quotes is that the Corinthians, in their celebration of the freedom found in Christ, have assumed that freedom means that they don't have to follow any rules at all, hence the statement "all things are lawful for me." In other words, they are free to live in whatever manner they please. They have an antinomian approach to Christianity, meaning that Christianity has nothing to do with rules and regulations.

Paul pushes back on the Corinthians' theology to help them see their newfound freedom in terms of opportunity *to do good*, rather than an opportunity to do whatever they want. Even if things are "lawful," are they helpful? In the midst of their so-called freedom, are they actually becoming "dominated" by their passions? (1 Corinthians 6:12). The Corinthians needed a better understanding of what it meant to be free in Christ. This theological confusion is manifested in the many controversies concerning sexual immorality within their church. Some within the church think that because they are free in Christ their sexual acts are no longer spiritually significant. It's nothing more than a natural, physical act—just like eating food is natural for the stomach (1 Corinthians 6:13). They are accepting a body and spirit separation that makes what they do with their bodies irrelevant to their religious commitments. But Paul rejects their notion that we have no spiritual claim on our bodies when we are free in Christ, for he says, "The body is not meant for sexual immorality, but for the Lord, and the Lord for the body" (1 Corinthians 6:13). This verse might sound odd to our ears. To say our bodies are "for the Lord" sounds a bit uncomfortable. However, Paul is trying to get them to understand how the spiritual and physical dimensions are intertwined. The physical act of sex has a spiritual dimension that should never be disregarded.

Paul's overall point is that a *laissez-faire* view of the body and sex does not recognize that freedom *in* Christ assumes we *belong* to Christ; after

all, that is what being "*in* Christ" means: we are *his*. Therefore, our
freedom does not release us from our moral obligations, rather in
some ways, it strengthens our moral obligations. Not only are our
bodies to be used for God's purposes, but they are actually a part
of Christ. Paul asks the church a rhetorical question with a note of
sarcasm in his voice: "Do you not know that your bodies are members
of Christ? Shall I then take the members of Christ and make them
members of a prostitute? Never!" (1 Corinthians 6:15). Paul is saying
that our faith in Christ unites us with Christ so that we are "members"
of him. He is the head and we are his body parts. Because our bodies
are joined to Christ through faith, Jesus has a large claim on our
bodies and how we operate within them. All the more, this very body
becomes the home of the Holy Spirit himself. Let us not corrupt that
which is the dwelling place of a holy God. Just as the Israelites cleansed
their community in order to house the temple of their God, so we too
must fight to purify ourselves as the temple of the Spirit. If the temple
is holy ground, our bodies are too. Paul offers an extremely high view
of your human body and its value. It is so precious that it is *sacred*. It
is set apart to the Lord. And because it is so sacred, it is not to be
taken lightly. If we treat expensive things with great care, how much
more should we treat holy things with the utmost care and caution?
Your body matters.

As we have seen, 1 Corinthians 6:12-20 is ultimately a discussion
of sexual purity. The command to be sexually pure is built upon a
theological basis that has wider implications for our discussion of self-
image. We must be careful that we do not make the same mistake as the

Corinthians when it comes to understanding who we are physically. Indeed, the social norm today is complete sexual liberty. There are almost no restrictions left on what sort of sexual activity is permissible. In the midst of a similar cultural current as the Corinthian church, we need to hear the words of Paul: *our bodies are not our own* (1 Corinthians 6:19). The Corinthians misunderstood Christian freedom to be the ability to do whatever they wanted with their bodies and feel no shame. Similarly today, Christian women often mistake the "empowerment" of Christian freedom to mean that their physical body has nothing to do with their spiritual commitments. Consequently, they think they can express their sexuality however they please. This is how we can make sense of statements like, "Your clothing says nothing about your character," or "Your sexuality has nothing to do with your faith." However, Paul labors to make this clear: not only were our souls bought on the cross by the blood of Christ, but our bodies were too. Therefore, just as God has a claim on your soul for his glory, so too he has a claim on your body for his glory. The gospel is not that which allows us to do whatever we want with our bodies; it actually lays a claim upon our bodies. You can see this logic in Paul's words: "for you were bought with a price. *So* glorify God in your body" (1 Corinthians 6:20). Because we are bought with a price (the gospel), we must glorify God with our bodies (submitting our physical bodies to God). The gospel and your body are not disconnected—not at all.

It is clear, then, that sexual looseness or promiscuous dress is not proper for the woman bought with such a high price. But what does it mean for our self-image? How does it change our mindset when we look in the mirror? This brings us back to our definition of beauty: *the ability of an object or form to communicate truth and/or realize goodness.* The purpose of your body is to communicate the goodness of God. In other words, your physical purpose is to "glorify God in your body." So when you look in the mirror and are disappointed with what you see, or when you long to have the body of the girl next to you and are endlessly dominated by insecurity, remember: you are not your own. Your physical body, despite its many flaws, is a glory machine for your Maker and Redeemer. And if that is your purpose, you can fulfill it much better by walking obediently than you can by having the perfect curves or being pimple-free. When we think of ourselves as belonging to God, our physical appearance becomes less about being attractive and more about being faithful. Indeed, our self-image stems from the belief that our bodies are holy ground because the Holy Spirit dwells within us. Your body has a much greater value and purpose than you could have ever imagined.

So what can we say about the controversial "my body, my choice"? Certainly we cannot fully concur. This does not mean that we think we can impose our desires on other people's bodies—absolutely not. The Christian does not think other people's bodies should be treated according to *our* choice. Rather, bodies should be treated according to *God's* choice. It means that God can impose his desires on our bodies (which he always does for our good). A better motto for the Christian woman might be, "my body, his glory."

REFLECTION **&** APPLICATION:

1. *What was the mistake the Corinthians made when thinking about the relationship between their spirits and their bodies? How do we make that same mistake today?*

2. *How is this passage an example of the Bible's very high view of our physical, bodily nature as humans?*

3. *What does it mean to "glorify God in your body"? Think of three specific ways you can glorify God in your body.*

MODESTY

TELL YOU:

"Women empowerment means celebrating our bodies and expressing ourselves through our clothing. Controlling what women wear is patriarchal and sexist."

READ 1 TIMOTHY 2

What God

TELLS YOU:

"Women should adorn themselves in respectable apparel, with modesty and self-control, not with braided hair and gold or pearls or costly attire, but with what is proper for women who profess godliness—with good works."

1 TIMOTHY 2:9-10

1 Timothy 2 is the Achilles' heel of the "biblical feminist" movement. In just a few verses, Paul exposes himself to be what our culture would call a misogynist, chauvinist, and oppressor of women. It is typical of Christian feminists today to tackle this beast of a passage by chalking it all up to context. They believe this portion of Paul's letter to Timothy is not a universal, God-ordained message. It is advice for certain people at a certain time and it really does not apply to us today in any direct way today. Certainly, there is a time and place for the contextualization of certain biblical commands. Rarely will hear Christians argue that we need to abstain from tattoos or piercings, which was a command to God's people in the Old Testament! Most biblical commentators, however, will suggest that this Old Testament command is no longer applicable to our modern world because of the development of the new covenant between God and man. Through obeying these commands, the people of Israel would set themselves apart as God's holy people. But we are not here to discuss tattoos and piercings. The point is that some biblical passages warrant an interpretation focused on context. The danger

for Christians today is to use context as a cop out for biblical ideas or commands we do not like. One must be careful to know when and why contextualization is appropriate when interpreting the Scriptures.

While this is not a book on hermeneutics (the study of interpreting biblical texts), it serves our purposes to understand that we ought to be wary of attributing passages that offend us to a purely contextual command. There are no signs in the text that Paul gives an exception. First, he says that he wants men to pray and to do away with anger and quarreling (1 Timothy 2:8). Then he says, *"likewise,"* women ought to dress a certain way. This "likewise" makes it clear that Paul's commandments are significantly connected. Just as it is proper for men of God to be temperate and slow to anger, so it is for women of God to be modest and self-controlled. None of us would want to say that the command to the men is not directly applicable to men today. Surely, we still want our men to pray and fight the urge to be aggressive and divisive. But we question the universality of the command for women to be modest because it frustrates our cultural sentiments. An arrogant, hot-headed man is labeled for his "toxic masculinity," so we applaud the Bible for its condemnation of it. Contrarily, promiscuity would never be identified as "toxic femininity" (indeed, no such phrase exists!), because we think modesty is oppressive and misogynistic. How are we to justify the universal nature of the command to men and yet limit the command to females purely due to Timothy's time and specific church? Even if it was a command meant only for Timothy's church, is there not still a principle behind this command that contradicts contemporary feminist ideology?

As we attempt to understand and apply 1 Timothy 2:9-10, we discover that Paul is not ignorant, sexist, or bigoted when discussing modesty, nor is he naive and primitive when giving Timothy these instructions for the church. We will also discover the command to women here is not limited to the women of Timothy's church in Ephesus. It seems clear that such an interpretation is motivated by our desires, rather than the textual evidence. Therefore, as we read and apply, may we trust that what originally may offend us, will turn out for our good, for our God knows better than we do.

Verse 9 begins with "likewise," which suggests that just as anger and quarreling are common temptations for Christian men, so too promiscuity and vanity are often temptations for Christian women. Neither anger nor promiscuity are a proper reflection of who we are in Christ. They are improper. The words Paul uses to describe the proper attire for a woman of God include "respectable," "modest," and "self-controlled" (1 Timothy 1:9). We may be tempted to think of knee-length skirts and condemned spaghetti straps when thinking of Christian modesty, but the words Paul associates with the term "modesty" remind us of a much broader understanding of the term. For Paul, modesty in dress is a physical manifestation of self-control. It is an expression of humility, prudence, temperance, and chastity. Let us consider some ways in which modesty reverses three sinful dispositions of our hearts: self-absorption, vanity, and promiscuity.

First, our sinful hearts are prone to self-absorption. We tend to fixate on ourselves. Sometimes our clothing can reflect a sinful mindset that says, "Look at me, look at me!" Conversely, modest dress is the expression of a self that is others-oriented. The person that dresses modestly is not asking for all eyes to be on them. It is a physical appearance that is unforthcoming and discreet. It does not draw so much attention to itself. It is not one of glitz and glamour. It does not beg for attention. That is why Paul contrasts modesty with fancy hair styles, extravagant jewelry, and expensive clothing (1 Timothy 2:9). An immodest way of dressing is all about impression. It begs to make a statement. It desires to be noticed. A lack of modesty ultimately reflects a heart of self-absorption. It reveals a heart too hungry for recognition and attention.

Secondly, immodest dress can reflect a lifestyle of luxury and excess. The grandiose and ostentatious clothing of women can be a reflection of a pretentious heart that clings to worldly wealth and accolades, therefore, clothing becomes a physical expression of high-class sophistication and affluence. Their dress becomes a way of asserting their worthiness or superiority in social settings. It associates themselves with a certain cultural status. I can remember in middle school being ashamed that my mother was going to buy me Bearpaws instead of Uggs. I was embarrassed to be seen in the off-brand, cheap version of the latest and greatest fashion trend. Without realizing, I was allowing my clothing to be a source of pride. So modest clothing is a way to present ourselves in humility instead of pride. Rather than using clothing to foster vanity, clothing should express humility.

Finally, immodest dress also reflects a heart disposed toward sexual promiscuity. Clothing that highlights the sexual nature of a woman's body becomes a form of seduction, whether we want to admit it or not. Glamorous clothing reflects a desire for attention, but it also can reflect a desire for *uncommitted, sexual attention*. Dressing in ways that are particularly "sexy" is considered improper for a woman of God by Paul because Christianity reserves sexual relationships to marriage. Therefore, public sexual expression is not empowering, but harmful. A woman's body is too sacred to be so accessible. Indeed, it is Paul's extremely high view of a woman's bodies that motivates his call to modesty, not a low view of them. When we consider these three issues related to modesty, we can see that clothing can reflect a heart of self-absorption, vanity, and promiscuity. On the contrary, modesty embodies a heart of self-forgetfulness, humility, and sexual restraint.

The claim that clothing is a physical expression of a disposition in our hearts is quite controversial. Some might respond in anger and conclude that defining a woman by her appearance and making assumptions about her character because of her clothing is the opposite of Christian love. While we would never want to define a person *purely* on the basis of their physical appearance, it is Paul, not us, that makes this connection between our apparel and our integrity. There is a "proper" way of dressing for the godly woman. This means that there is a fitting or appropriate physical expression of godliness in our clothing and there are certain ways of dressing that are an inconsistent expression of godliness in our clothing. By saying this, Paul assumes that our choice of clothing reflects our heart in some meaningful way. Otherwise, he would not touch on it at all. But when we take Paul seriously, we realize that this is the basis of all Christian ethics. Commendable actions reflect holy desires of the heart, and condemnable actions express unholy desires of the heart. Our outward decisions are intimately connected with our inward wishes, so why would clothing be excluded from that category?

The New Testament offers us an extremely counter-cultural way to reinforce our identity as God's precious, redeemed people. One way in which we can live out, reinforce, and express who we are as Christian women is through modesty. Clothing is a way in which we declare and embrace a modesty that goes far beyond covering up our cleavage (though surely it includes that). It turns out that modesty is the truest form of self-expression for the Christian. Culture wants to tell you that wearing little to no clothing is a form of innocent self-expression and body confidence. In reality, the Bible would lead us to believe that it is the physical expression of a lust for attention. By calling this promiscuous way of clothing "self-expression," culture admits that our clothing has something important to do with our identity. What they will not concede is that promiscuity is the expression of a rebellious and egotistical self. They insist that it is an expression of confidence and self-celebration that is proper for the empowered women. But if that is what empowerment looks like, the Christian woman should want nothing of it. Empowerment does not mean exaltation, it means humility. And so when you go to dress yourself in the morning, there is no need to be legalistic nor is there a need to try to present yourself in an unappealing way. But there is a need to consider whether or not your clothing reflects a heart of humility and love or a need for attention and to be seen as attractive.

REFLECTION & APPLICATION:

1. *How does Paul view the connection between our clothing and our character? How does this conflict with popular opinion today?*

2. *Purity culture in the church receives criticism for making unnecessarily strict rules, being legalistic, and even making women feel responsible for men's lustful hearts. How does this text on modesty give us a broader understanding of the Christian woman's obligation to modesty? How can that help keep us away from being legalistic when it comes to modesty?*

3. *What are three things you should consider before wearing an outfit in public? Can you see any ways in which you have allowed your clothing to foster self-absorption, vanity, or promiscuity? How can you change that?*

Deceptive

BEAUTY

What They

TELL YOU:

"You are beautiful, inside and out."

READ ISAIAH 3

What God

TELLS YOU:

"In that day the Lord will take away the finery of the anklets, the headbands, and the crescents; the pendants, the bracelets, and the scarves; the headdresses, the armlets, the sashes, the perfume boxes, and the amulets; the signet rings and nose rings; the festal robes, the mantles, the cloaks, and the handbags; the mirrors, the linen garments, the turbans, and the veils. Instead of perfume there will be rottenness; and instead of a belt, a rope; and instead of well-set hair, baldness; and instead of a rich robe, a skirt of sackcloth, and branding instead of beauty."

ISAIAH 3:18-24

"Charm is deceitful, and beauty is vain, but a woman who fears the LORD is to be praised."

PROVERBS 31:30

In Isaiah 3, the Lord stands to contend against his wayward people (Isaiah 3:13). The language reminds us of a courtroom scene wherein the accuser boldly comes after the accused. God charges his covenant people with a myriad of offenses: words and deeds that defy the glorious presence of the Lord (Isaiah 3:8), celebration of their disobedience (Isaiah 3:9), and a complete disregard (even "devouring") of the poor (Isaiah 3:14-15). As the list of abominations goes on, Isaiah slows down for a moment to specifically reflect on the women of Jerusalem and how they contribute to the situation at hand. However, these women are apparently quite confident. The description of verses 16-17 seems comparable to a scene in a modern-day chick flick with a bunch of hot girls walking in slow motion through high school hallways as boys whistle and drool. They see the boys' eyes fixated upon them as they walk by and hit them with the smize and a flirty battering of their eyelashes. Their hips move with just enough *oomph* that you can't help but notice their figure. Applying their lip gloss and smacking their lips, they have all the men gawking. Turns out this stereotype was around long before chick flicks. With their heads held high, seduction in their eyes, necks adorned with expensive jewelry, and footsteps that strut with utter confidence, these women of Zion are the prototype for the popular girls in our favorite high school movies.

This stereotype may be so far from how you see yourself. You may not identify at all with this kind of caricature. If this *Mean Girls-esque* image isn't working for you, imagine our society's ultimate, independent woman. She is attractive, curvy, confident, bold, stylish, and assertive. *She don't need no man.* She is a woman who does it all. She is successful in her career, knows her value, puts herself first, and is not afraid to be who she is. She is the image of the empowered woman here in the West. Now do you see the appeal? Maybe you don't want to be the woman running in slow motion on the beach in *Baywatch*, but the idea of being self-assured, self-reliant, and sexy—all at the same time—is certainly appealing. Sadly, that ideal may not be too far from the description of the women in Isaiah 3. This façade of confidence mixed with sexual allure and fancy clothes is what women today often call "empowerment." What our culture has exalted as the essence of womanhood, Isaiah seems to condemn. But why? Why does the outward appearance of the women in Jerusalem have anything to do with their inward character?

Our culture has a natural disgust for those who think your dress code has anything to do with your character. Nonetheless, society does not completely disconnect our inner selves from our self-presentation. This belief is connected to our understanding of empowerment.

Society views empowerment as expressing yourself and your sexuality in any way you please. One form of empowerment is self-expression and celebration through our clothing. It's about wearing whatever makes you feel confident. Although clothing and self-presentation are forms of self-expression and self-confidence, they cannot tell you about someone's integrity. So in today's common thinking, *clothing does make a statement about you, but that statement has nothing to do with your moral goodness.*

When we read this passage in Isaiah, however, it suggests otherwise. As Isaiah describes the appearance of these women, the reflection of their character unfolds. Isaiah confirms our belief that clothing communicates something about ourselves, but he rejects our belief that clothing never reflects our character. While clothing is certainly not the sole and most accurate indicator of a person's integrity, it can sometimes be indicative. That is why Isaiah takes so much time to describe the physical appearance of these women. The way they present themselves deeply connects with who they think they are. That is why verse 16 connects a condition of their heart (arrogance) with physical presentation (their walk, their eyes, their clothing). Since their presentation of their physical self reflects the corruption of their hearts, they are condemned for it. It is these very women—the empowered, beautiful, and confident women of verses 16-17—who will end up in the situation of verses 19-23. What a harsh turn of events! Not forever will their perverse hearts be masked with an appearance of glory. Their current looks are a mere deception. Their outward appearance of pride and power is a mirage that will soon fade and give way to a horrifying reality.

Proverbs 11:22 seems pertinent to this discussion: "Like a gold ring in a pig's snout is a beautiful woman without discretion." A woman with an attractive outward appearance but a foolish heart is analogous to a pig playing dress up. You can slap some lipstick on a pig, but it's still a pig. That might sound harsh, but we need to hear it. It tells us something about physical beauty in our broken world. Ever since the fall, the beauty that was created to manifest the glory of its Creator is now often used as a mask for the corrupted creation. Because of this, the beauty in our sinful world often has a deceptive nature. Physical attractiveness becomes a sort of pseudo-beauty in that it *communicates the glory of God while also distorting the glory of God*. It communicates the glory of God in showcasing his ability to make physically glorious things. It shows God's handiwork as an artist through the physically beautiful things he crafts. When we see a stunningly beautiful woman, we are gazing into God's artistry. But it also distorts the glory of God because the person's outward appearance is inconsistent with her ugly spirit. In that sense, her physical appearance is a lie. The person who was to image God both in her physical glory and her spiritual submission has settled for good looks instead of good character—and one is much more important than the other. Not only is one more important, but one is in her control while the other is not. She is responsible for her moral character, but is not responsible for breaking out or having crooked teeth. When women flaunt features considered more attractive than others, it perpetuates the lie that physical goods are more important than spiritual goods. Beauty, which has been a communicative tool for God's glory since before the fall, now has the capacity to distort God's glory in women who show off their "sexy" features with no regard to the God who fearfully and wonderfully crafted their physical bodies.

Let's look at why Proverbs 31:30 claims that "charm is deceitful and beauty is vain." Beauty is all about communicating who God is. Yet, we experience a contradiction when physical beauty and spiritual ugliness exist simultaneously. The cure for such beautiful deception, according to Proverbs 31:30, is fear of the Lord, something the women from Isaiah's day lacked—and something women today lack, too. Confidence is not always key. The fear of the Lord is the beginning of all wisdom, and therefore, is the beginning of understanding what beauty truly is. Do not let outward appearances fool you; God looks at the heart (1 Samuel 16:7). God looks at the heart because, in a broken sinful world, our physical goodness does not correspond to our spiritual goodness. One day, God will take away the physical masks of beauty or flaws and assign us a physical form worthy of our corruption. For those who are inwardly cleansed by the blood of Christ, an imperishable body of glory they shall receive (1 Corinthians 15:42-43). Those who refuse the purifying work of Christ will end up with a body that is just as corrupt as their heart. This was the message of Isaiah to the women who took pride in their physical attractiveness.

It seems that the pursuit of beauty for the Christian woman must seek to undo its potential for deception. Physically beautiful things are not the problem in and of themselves. The biblical view of beauty we have defended is actually a very high view of beauty. Beauty is one of the most powerful ways God communicates himself to us. But how do we reconcile that view of beauty with Proverbs 31:30? In a fallen world, physical beauty has the potential to deceive. This is the exact opposite of what beauty was originally meant to do. Beauty should reveal the truth to us. The pig with a ring on its snout does the opposite of truth-telling; it communicates a lie. The women of Jerusalem perpetuated a lie through their physical appearance. If we maintain that beauty is intimately connected with communicating truth, we must strive to make beautiful things that are not deceiving nor misleading. Beauty is not a cover-up for that which is ultimately ugly. We should not seek fraudulent beauty. We must never let beauty turn out to be a scam. We want physical beauty to be a true portrayal of the greater, spiritual beauty. We will discuss later on.

REFLECTION & APPLICATION:

1. *Physical beauty is often deceptive because it masks spiritual ugliness. Does this mean that every attractive woman is particularly sinful because her physical body is a mask for her sinful heart? No! What is the difference between simply being physically attractive and presenting yourself as the women do in Isaiah 3? How could that apply to us today?*

2. *God's final judgment will one day give us a physical form that is consistent with our spiritual state, but for now, in this broken world, our physical appearance does not have anything to do with our worth, value, or our character. Why is this an important message for women today (both those who are confident in their looks and those who are insecure about their looks)?*

3. *Christians should pursue beauty as a way of communicating truth; therefore, we should be wary of beauty that exalts anything sinful. How does this apply to the kind of art we interact within our daily lives? Whether photography, poetry, literature, movies, or music, these art forms use artistry to communicate to us, and therefore, are using beauty as a mask for ultimately ugly concepts. This tempts us to delight in sinful things because beautiful things often cause enjoyment or satisfaction. Can you think of any art you enjoy that communicates or even exalts bad things?*

VAINGLORY

What They

TELL YOU:

"Self-confidence means celebrating your body."

READ EZEKIEL 16

What God

TELLS YOU:

"And your renown went forth among the nations because of your beauty, for it was perfect through the splendor that I had bestowed on you, declares the Lord God. But you trusted in your beauty and played the whore because of your renown and lavished your whorings on any passerby; your beauty became his."

EZEKIEL 16:14-15

E zekiel 16 tells the story of Israel's covenant infidelity. It begins
with a history lesson and a marriage metaphor. God reminds
the city of Jerusalem of her sad beginnings. Long before
God established his people in Jerusalem, it was a pathetic city owned
but not cared for by the pagan Amorites who inhabited the land.
He describes the city as a neglected baby. She was born to heartless
parents who abandoned their child (Ezekiel 16:5). Baby Jerusalem
was not given the basic provisions that a child needed (Ezekiel 16:4).
The passage continues in the metaphor of Jerusalem as a growing
young woman, saying that no one had compassion on her and no
one pitied her desperate condition. But the Lord looked upon the
helpless woman. It was he who rescued her and committed himself to
her. He established a covenant of marriage with her and vowed to be
faithful to her (Ezekiel 16:8). Not only that, but he lavished upon her
luxurious goods. He clothed her with embroidered linens and covered
her in fine leather (Ezekiel 16:10). He showered her with expensive
jewelry and even adorned her with a beautiful crown. Indeed, the once

helpless baby that grew into a neglected young woman has now become "exceedingly beautiful," even advancing to royalty (Ezekiel 16:13).

Then comes the verses that we will focus on today: the lavished wife becomes renowned among the nations for her beauty (Ezekiel 16:14). The other nations cannot help but notice her excellence and grandeur. Her beauty was deemed perfect, but only through the gracious provision of her compassionate husband, for he was the one who bestowed this splendor upon her (Ezekiel 16:14). But this great gift became an opportunity for pride. The fame of beauty tempted the pride-sensitive heart of God's covenant partner (the city of Jerusalem) just like it did to Eve in the Garden. Their beauty led them to trust in themselves and eventually to infidelity. The beautiful woman cheats on her Husband—the one who gave her everything he had. She scorns the Husband who loved her when no one else did, and she uses his gifts to flaunt her independence. Thus the adorned wife becomes an arrogant whore. She gave to random men the gift of beauty she received from her compassionate husband (Ezekiel 16:15).

This passage in Ezekiel clues us into another detrimental potential in physical beauty. Not only can it be deceptive, but it is also an open doorway to pride. The human heart tends to take gifts and use them as opportunities for self-exaltation. Jerusalem allowed the blessing of her God to give her an ego boost. She seemed to forget that her beauty was not of herself, but its source was from another. We often do the same thing. In reality, your beautiful eyes have nothing to do with your greatness. They are a creation of the Creator, freely given to you.

Ultimately, your beautiful figure, your delightful smile, your luscious hair, or your stunning complexion is more reflective of who your Creator is than who you are. They are manifestations of his glorious workmanship. Not only his artistry, but his compassion on you, and his desire to adorn you. Not only were the people God's creation, but they were his covenant partners in whom he delighted (that is why we see the metaphor of marriage). Their beauty was an indicator of the glory of their Maker and the blessing of their Lord.

The piece of art does not take pride in itself. It testifies to the glory of the artist. No one praises a painting for being beautiful. They praise the artist. Even if the painting had a life of its own, it would not presume to praise itself when it is simply a product of another's artistry. However, our tainted hearts are prone to take that which was made for the glory of God and use it for the glory of the self. We use physical attractiveness as an opportunity to get attention, significance, and worth, just as the people did in Ezekiel 16. They allowed the fame and fortune of beauty to deceive them into believing they were great; in reality, it was their God who was great. Just as we have the sinful tendency to boast in a freely given salvation, we also have the tendency to boast in the freely given gift of beauty. Neither your salvation nor your beauty has anything to do with your worthiness. Both are free, undeserved gifts of the Creator. Culture insists that being "beautiful" according to society's standards does not determine your worth. But culture does not fix our insecurity by disconnecting our worth from our physical appearance; rather, we must convince ourselves that we are beautiful even if society does not think so. And so we come up with statements like "all bodies are bikini bodies" to try to comfort those who feel unworthy due to their physical appearance. But in reality, we just need to separate our physical attractiveness from our worth completely. You do not have to think your body is a bikini body. Allowing the shape of our body to relate to our sense of self is dangerous. Culture recognizes that when it comes to low self-esteem. It acknowledges that you cannot let your appearance lead you to a lack of self-worth. But culture is not consistent. It does not remind us that we cannot let our appearance lead us to a greater sense of self-worth. On the internet and by celebrities, we are constantly warned to never let our appearance make us insecure (and rightly so), but we are never warned to never let our appearance make us proud. We need to realize that our appearance and our worth are not connected at all. When we let our physical beauty lead us to pride (just as when we let it lead to insecurity), we forget that very important truth, and God is not pleased with it. Beauty should never serve as a way to exalt ourselves.

Again, this takes us back to a biblical definition of beauty. If beauty is all about communicating God's goodness and truth, then beauty used for the exaltation of the self is an abomination. Beauty is always meant to be a lens through which we see God. *Beauty is meant to be "seen through."* It is a window into glory. But if what people see when they look through the window of beauty is just me, then beauty has failed its purpose. You are meant to be seen through, not in a demeaning way, but in an empowering way. This is what it means to be an image-bearer. This means our purpose is to point to another. Our nature is a symbol of something greater. Being an image of God means being a reflection of God. A reflection is dependent on what it reflects. So if our beauty does not reflect who God is, it is not beauty at all.

What might this mean for our lives today? *It means that what culture calls self-confidence or self-expression is often just pride.* Posting beach pictures because we are confident in our bodies is usually just a feat of self-absorption. It forgets that our beauty is not something we should take responsibility for. The only sense in which body boasting is "brave" is that it is quite brave to take credit for something you primarily have no control over. It is foolish bravery. Indeed many women work hard to get their bodies in a place that they are happy with, but by exalting ourselves for getting in shape, we might make the girl who can't seem to lose a few pounds feel inadequate. We need to remember we have no say in a large part of our bodies' appearance. So to make our bodily appearance a source of pride does not really make sense. And because we allow beauty to be an opportunity for pride, we also allow lack of beauty to be a source of worthlessness. If you are to be proud of the parts of your body you like, it makes sense that you end up ashamed of the parts of your body you don't like. What if we removed worth and value completely from our physical appearance? What if we let physical beauty be neither an opportunity for pride nor insecurity? Instead, what if we let beauty be a way in which God communicates truth to us? For those of us who, unlike the arrogant city of Jerusalem, don't feel beautiful, we tend to run and hide. We do not want to be seen. For those of us who do feel beautiful, we boast and are hungry to be seen. Both are mistakes. Acknowledging that we are all a mixture of beauty and ugliness will teach us that we should not be invisible, nor should we be center stage. The degree of physical beauty has nothing to do with your identity: it is simply a gift of God. But there is a much greater gift of God, and it is not physical beauty. It is spiritual beauty. So let us bask in the good gifts God gives and not make them about ourselves. And let us pursue the greatest kind of beauty: the gift of spiritual renewal.

REFLECTION & APPLICATION:

1. *Physical beauty is a gift. It is not something that relates to our worth or identity. How can you present yourself in such a way that reminds you and others that beauty should not be a source of self-esteem? How do we sometimes accidentally reinforce that lie by the way we talk about others and to others (whether that be by complimenting their shape or by insulting it)?*

2. *Physical beauty can instill pride in the sinful heart. When we draw attention to our appearance, we take advantage of it and forsake God in the process. How do you draw attention using your appearance? Or, the opposite extreme, how do you use your physical appearance to hide from attention? Are your clothes saying "look at me!" or are they saying "I am invisible?" Both are distortions of the image of God in you. Consider how you can correct those mindsets and how you can use your clothes to reinforce the correct mindset.*

3.   *Boasting about our bodies isn't brave. It is foolish. Can you think of ways social media teaches us to boast in our appearance? How can you fight that?*

Unseen

BEAUTY

What They

TELL YOU:

"Do whatever it takes to be confident in your own skin."

READ 1 PETER 3

What God

TELLS YOU:

"Do not let your adorning be external—the braiding of hair and the putting on of gold jewelry, or the clothing you wear—but let your adorning be the hidden person of the heart with the imperishable beauty of a gentle and quiet spirit, which in God's sight is very precious."

1 PETER 3:3-4

We have seen how physical beauty, in a broken world, actually has the ability to do the opposite of what beauty was meant to do. If beauty is a powerful, artistic way of communicating the goodness and glory of God, then our physical beauty can only accomplish that task in a distorted way. And this is not just because we are overweight or have frizzy hair. It is because our physical beauty can so often become a machine for self-glorification rather than God-glorification. In a self-obsessed world, we find a way to take that which God has purposed for his glory and make it into that which is used for our glory. This is how the biblical Christian can have both a very high view of beauty while also have a somewhat suspicious view of beauty. In some ways, the biblical tradition exalts beauty to a position that is far beyond that which the world would ever dare designate to it. The Bible sees beauty as an expression of God's nature, and therefore, it is highly sacred and most definitely to be sought after. On the other hand, the Bible is highly critical of the ways in which physical beauty is so often a source of deception, lust, and pride in our world. The Bible warns us of the dangers of physical beauty in a world such as ours and condemns those who allow their beautiful appearance to be a mask for their ugly character. So how should the Christian woman view beauty? Should she pursue it? Or should she forsake it?

Peter offers us a nuanced view of beauty in his letter to a group of believers scattered in the Dispersion. In chapter 3, Peter instructs the wives within the church, specifically wives who may be married to an unbelieving husband. The wives are called to respect their husband's role as leader and submit themselves to him, even though his leadership is likely less than worthy of it. Peter's reasoning for this approach is evangelical. He believes that a wife who treats her husband with love and respect has the power to communicate the gospel to him more vividly than a preacher or teacher can with words and intellect. When the husband sees the lifestyle of his wife, he will be compelled towards the message of the gospel (I Peter 3:1-2). And so it is by her conduct that a wife might bring her husband to faith. It cannot be a coincidence that this command to conduct a life that communicates the glory of the gospel is paired with a command about beauty. This is because beauty is essentially about powerful communication—illuminating the nature of God. Beauty is a form of communication that is uniquely vivid in how it realizes God's goodness to us. Beautiful things have a way of gripping us. So Peter is saying that a beautiful life is an incredibly persuasive way of spreading the gospel. In this sense, the women of the church ought always to pursue beauty, devoting their lives to living beautifully and being living, breathing expressions of the Good News of Jesus. Peter is aware of the temptation for many women to make beauty about being physically appealing or attractive. Peter knows that many women are more worried about how their physical appearance communicates something about themselves rather than how their character communicates something about God. And for this reason, Peter instructs them to not allow for their "adorning" to be external, but rather internal (1 Peter 3:4). It is the beauty of character that should be their primary pursuit. It is our flesh that wants to make beauty all about physical appearance. But it is much more than that. Remember the deed that Jesus proclaimed "beautiful"? It was a woman anointing him for burial. Her act was beautiful because it powerfully communicated the Good News. The beauty we must seek after is not merely a physical condition. The pursuit of beauty for the Christian woman is more than physical; it is spiritual. It is a way of life that seeks to illuminate the gospel just as the woman in Bethany did with her anointing oil.

Peter continues to describe this beauty as that which is of the "hidden person of the heart" who has a "gentle and quiet spirit" (1 Peter 3:4). This type of beauty does not draw attention to itself through fancy hair updos and sparkly jewelry; it is much more subtle. It is a beauty that captivates souls by giving them a taste of the imperishable beauty of glory. That is the beauty that is "precious in God's sight" (1 Peter 3:4). It is the beauty of the fruit of the Spirit. It is the beauty of humility. By associating beauty with a "gentle and quiet spirit," Peter fights against the other common temptation for women in their pursuit of beauty. We tend to partner beauty with vanity and pride. Self-confidence and self-assuredness are a big part of beauty today.

But our godly nature ought to partner beauty with humility because one of the most spectacular ways we can communicate the gospel to people is by mimicking the humility of Christ. So if beauty is all about communicating who God is, humility will always play an important role. By elaborating on his view of beauty, Peter cautions the women of the church to not chase after physical exaltation and vanity when they seek after beauty.

So we understand that the beauty of character should take precedence over the beauty of the body in the Christian life. Not a huge surprise there. But is physical beauty a bad thing? When Peter says "do not let your adorning be external," is he implying we cannot look pretty? Is he saying we have to throw out our foundation, concealer, skin-care serums, and eyeshadow palette? Not necessarily. Some commentators translate this passage as saying that our adorning should not be *merely* external. The word "merely" is not in the original Greek text, but the commentators are making an interpretative call by including it. They may recognize that the Scriptures do not condemn physical beauty, but they warn of its potential dangers. Peter knows that physical forms can "declare the glory of God" just like the heavens can (Psalm 19:1). But he also knows that physical beauty is never a sure sign of godliness. Therefore, he encourages the women of God to seek after an adorning that is far superior to physical attractiveness. The word translated "adorning" is *kosmos*, the same word often translated "world" in Greek. It refers to the world or the universe or the worldly affairs within it, but it can also refer to the harmonious order of the world. This is why our term "cosmetic" comes from the Greek *kosmos*. Cosmetic refers to the beauty of the created order. In this sense, the word can even refer to that which embellishes or decorates. Adorning refers to that which embellishes you. It is what beautifies you or distinguishes you. In other words, what do people notice about you, oh woman of God? Do they notice your great body, your gorgeous eyes, or your fantastic sense of style? Or do they notice your sacrificial love and commitment to Christ? The goal is not to be pretty, it is to be Christ-like. If our clothing sends the message that we are more concerned with our appearance than our character, then we are doing something wrong. Our clothing ought to be a daily reminder of the gracious salvation of Jesus Christ, who clothes our nakedness and covers our shame.

REFLECTION **&** APPLICATION:

1. *How do the verses in this text reinforce the belief that beauty is all about communicating something? Think about verses 1 Peter 3:1-2 and how they connect to verses 3-4. Both verses talk about how we can communicate something true and good.*

2. *How does the Bible give us a sacred and a suspicious view of beauty? How does Psalm 19:1 give us the sacred view of beauty? How does Proverbs 11:22 give us the suspicious view of beauty?*

3. *How does Peter balance these two different views of beauty? How should Christian women pursue beauty in life?*

Three Spiritual Disciplines
to Embrace a Biblical View
of Beauty:

1. Don't look in the mirror for one whole day

2. Fast from social media

3. Practice modesty in a new way

WEEK FIVE

The

FUTURE

Self

Everything is Not

AS IT SEEMS

TELL YOU:

"Just because we have tummy rolls and chafing thighs doesn't mean we need fixed. You don't need to be fixed. Embrace your body as it is."

READ 2 CORINTHIANS 4

What God

TELLS YOU:

"So we do not lose heart. Though our outer self is wasting away, our inner self is being renewed day by day. For this light momentary affliction is preparing for us an eternal weight of glory beyond all comparison, as we look not to the things that are seen but to the things that are unseen. For the things that are seen are transient, but the things that are unseen are eternal."

2 CORINTHIANS 4:16-18

In 2 Corinthians 4, Paul clarifies the nature of his ministry as an apostle of Christ Jesus. His goal is not to proclaim himself, but to make himself a servant to proclaim Christ (2 Corinthians 4:5). He calls the Good News of Jesus the "treasure" that he and the rest of the apostles have in "jars of clay" (2 Corinthians 4:7). They only have a restricted amount of this treasure to share, for they are not the true owners of this gospel. They are limited so that God may be shown to be unlimited. He is the one to whom all the power belongs. Furthermore, they are often weak in afflictions and persecutions, following in their Master's footsteps of suffering, declaring his life, death, and resurrection to all the world. And even though they are afflicted, they are not crushed, and though they are perplexed, they are not driven to despair. They are indeed persecuted, but they are not forsaken. They have been struck down but never destroyed. And they do all this for the sake of proclaiming the truth of the gospel (2 Corinthians 4:8-11). They do it for the sake of the church. They do it for the sake of the glory of God.

Knowing their labor is not in vain, they do not lose heart. In the midst of their afflictions, they remind the church of an important truth: Everything is not what it seems. It may appear as though they are wasting away, but in actuality, they are being renewed day by day (2 Corinthians 4:16). It may seem as though the weight of their affliction is unbearable, but it cannot compare with the weight of glory they will soon receive. Indeed, their outward appearance plays the same trick as the cross did. That which looks disgusting is actually an instrument for glory. That which seems to degrade is, in truth, making us whole. That which appears to bring death is really bringing life. And all the more, that which should have been ugly, God is making beautiful.

If we remind ourselves of the biblical definition of beauty, we can better understand how God can make something we think is ugly into something beautiful. Beauty includes all the forms that communicate the truth and goodness of God in powerful ways. So what might at first seem extremely ugly to us—a man dying on a cross—has become the epitome of beauty because it is the singular event of history that communicates the truth and goodness of God most vividly to us. For that reason, it is arguably the most beautiful moment in history to date. Paul understands this and will not allow his unseemly—even humiliated—outward appearance to discourage him. He is aware that the gospel is the story of God making beauty out of ugliness. He is aware that Jesus' modest appearance in human flesh and his gruesome appearance on the cross were the path to greatness. Paul clings to the hope that one day his outward appearance will be that which is fitting of his inward state. His body will one day reflect the glory of

Christ. Jesus was emptied of glory and took upon himself the form of a servant, but now is glorified in a heavenly resurrected body. As his follower, Paul will also endure scorn and humiliation during his earthly habitation but will one day enjoy a resurrected body free from all infirmities. Paul bears the semblance of the crucified God in his earthly ministry, but in the coming age, he will reflect the majesty and grandeur of the risen King.

This *truth* offers two important insights regarding our current self and our future self. The first is that our current self, in its weakness and often undesirable appearance, is a machine for God's glory. The second insight is that the future self makes the current struggle worth it. Paul calls his daily persecutions and sufferings a "light and momentary affliction" (2 Corinthians 4:17). Why? Because those afflictions are preparing him for "an eternal weight of glory beyond all comparison" (2 Corinthians 4:17). In light of eternal glory, the current struggle is merely light and momentary. It is worth it. In Hebrews 12, the author tells us that it was "for the joy that was set before him" that Christ "endured the cross, despising the shame" (Hebrews 12:2). How does this fit with Paul's message in 2 Corinthians 4? It means that Jesus' appearance and experience of shame on the cross were worth it and even became beautiful and glorious because of what was on the other side. And so it is with Paul. And so it ought to be with us. We can endure the physical shame of our earthly lives as we look forward to the joy that is set before us, indeed the "eternal weight of glory beyond all comparison" that is set before us.

Paul will not be discouraged by his weakened and tired body. He does not lose heart as his outward self wastes away, but he also does not long to stay in his body as it is. He continues this thought in the next few verses saying that he "groans" in his "tent," [his mortal body], and longs to put on his heavenly dwelling [his resurrected body] (2 Corinthians 5:2). So in one sense, Paul is content with his current struggles, but on the other hand, he longs for that which is better. What does this mean? It means that *our future self creates a tension in our current self*. In one sense, we embrace this stage of shame. We carry the death of Christ in our bodies. We can find joy in the reality that though our appearance is wasting away, it is still a machine for God's glory. However, we also long for our new appearance. An appearance that is proper for the one whom God has made his child. An appearance with the glory that is fitting for one who is the image of God. This means that we do not have to celebrate every one of our flaws, nor do we have to love every physical feature we have. We do not have to convince ourselves that flaws are beautiful. We do not have to convince ourselves that we are perfect the way we are. We do not have to preach to ourselves that "we don't need fixed." Paul knows his physical body is not perfect, so he longs for a better one: his heavenly body. We can do the same thing. And it doesn't mean that we hate ourselves or shame ourselves. It just means that we do not avoid the fact that there are plenty of things about our current self, spiritual and physical, that could use an upgrade. Paul finds contentment in his imperfect physical body because in it, he can imitate the love of Christ on the cross, but he nonetheless longs to put on the greater body, rid of all weaknesses and infirmities.

But can Paul's contentment in his physical suffering and disfigurement really be a model for us when we are upset with a pimple or disappointed by our weight? Paul is being physically marred for the sake of spreading the gospel. We are just going through puberty. Paul's body bears shame because he is living with complete devotion to Christ. We bear shame because we are unsatisfied with our attractiveness. And certainly, it seems almost blasphemous to compare our physical flaws with the physical shame of Christ on the cross. Jesus endured physical disfigurement before he received glory, but comparing our acne and frizzy hair to that seems ridiculous. So does Paul's statement here really apply to us today as we struggle with body image? I think it does. If Paul can consider his mutilated body to be merely a "light momentary affliction," *how much more* can we consider our physical flaws and blemishes as light and momentary afflictions. If Jesus can endure whippings and physical humiliation for the joy set before him, how much more can we endure our less-than-perfect appearance for the joy set before us? If Paul can look to things unseen in the face of serious physical suffering, you can look to things unseen when faced with discontentment with your body. If Paul can see that physical humiliation has a way of communicating the transforming power of the cross, then you too can rest assured that each wrinkle and stretch mark is a way that God communicates his will to make that which is ugly into something beautiful. You do not have to celebrate all your flaws. You can long for the day that God will replace your shameful body with a body of glory. But you can also take joy this very day in the fact that your flawed appearance can be a vessel for God's glory.

Future glory teaches us to find joy in our current state of lowliness as it prepares us for the glory to come. While at the same time, we will never be fully satisfied with it because we know something better is on the way. Christ endured the cross knowing that God was making something beautiful out of it, but he did not stay in the grave. He now sits at the right hand of the throne of God in glory. Therefore, Christ both embraced his ministry of shame and yet also was not fulfilled until he reached glory. You must also strive to see how God is making things beautiful that make you feel are ugly all while pressing on to the day wherein you will receive a body of complete and utter splendor. The future self makes our current self a joyful and hopeful self.

REFLECTION & APPLICATION:

1. What gives Paul hope in the face of physical deterioration? How does our culture's desire to look young and emphasize anti-aging contradict what Paul teaches us here?

2. Why is the statement "everything is not as it seems" true when it comes to our physical bodies and appearance?

3. How does our future self inform our current self? How does the end of the story help us endure and even find joy in the current part of the story?

Reflective

BEAUTY

What They

TELL YOU:

"Beauty means being independent."

READ 2 CORINTHIANS 3

What God

TELLS YOU:

"And we all, with unveiled face, beholding the glory of the Lord, are being transformed into the same image from one degree of glory to another."

2 CORINTHIANS 3:18

"But our citizenship is in heaven, and from it we await a Savior, the Lord Jesus Christ, who will transform our lowly body to be like his glorious body, by the power that enables him even to subject all things to himself."

PHILIPPIANS 3:20-21

2 Corinthians chapter 3 is a very dense passage. We do not have the space to deal with all its richness here, but we will focus our attention on one particular theme: glory. Paul begins contrasting the old and new covenants (covenants are ways in which we can interact with and relate to God); both covenants are "ministries of glory" (2 Corinthians 3:7). He thinks back to the establishment of the covenant after the Exodus. After spending forty days on Mount Sinai "talking with God" (Exodus 34:29), Moses descends from the mountain glowing. His face shone so brightly that the people of Israel could not gaze upon it. Have you ever tried to stare straight into the sun? Think of it like that. Moses' appearance was so striking that it was frightening—so frightening that he covered it with a veil. Paul brings up this particular story to teach us how much better the new covenant is. If the temporal, imperfect covenant—which ultimately brought condemnation—came with such glory that mankind couldn't even look upon it, how much more glorious will the everlasting, perfect covenant be—which ultimately brings righteousness (2 Corinthians

3:7)?[1] If an inferior covenant had so much glory, imagine what glory this new and better covenant will have; it will far surpass the glory of the old.

Because of the superior glory of this new covenant—the covenant established by faith in Christ—we need not be bashful like Moses who covered his face that "Israelites might not gaze at the outcome of what was being brought to an end" (2 Corinthians 3:13). Instead, we ought to be bold. We need not put a veil over our faces to hide the glory being wrought within us. We need not cover up the outcome of the new and greater covenant of Christ. Rather, Paul says that "we all, with unveiled face, beholding the glory of the Lord, are being transformed into the same image from one degree of glory to another" (2 Corinthians 3:18). Like Moses, when we behold the glory of the Lord, we are transformed. But unlike Moses, we have the opportunity in Christ to do so with uncovered faces and therefore, be continually climbing the ladder of glory all the way to eternity.

There are so many questions we could ask of this text, but one point especially serves our purpose in understanding our future self—and how we live into that self today. This passage goes back to the original purpose of humanity: to *be* the image of God. Mankind was made to

---

1   "The psalmist rightly calls the law of God "perfect" (Psalm 19:7), yet the writer of Hebrews states the law of God "made nothing perfect" (Hebrews 7:19) and God brought about a "better covenant." Therefore, the law was perfect in its *nature*, but imperfect in its *results*. It perfectly displayed God's righteousness, but it could not make man righteous. See also Norman Geisler, *When Critics Ask: A Popular Handbook on Bible Difficulties* (Wheaton, IL: Victor Books, 1992), 24.

reflect God's goodness, kingship, and glory as his representatives on earth. This story of Moses might seem like a partial restoration of the image of God. As Moses spends time in the presence of the Lord, he begins to reflect the Lord's glory. When he comes down the mountain, his shining face is a representation of the glory of Yahweh. Moses is living into his purpose to image God. What Paul has in mind in 2 Corinthians will be the complete restoration of the image of God. In Christ, believers can behold the glory of God and begin to reflect that glory. This means that *transformation comes by beholding our God*. Transformation is a process fueled by our gazing upon his majesty. As we behold his glory, we begin to reflect his glory. And as we reflect his glory, we restore the image of God. We become who we were meant to be. And all the more, we become the epitome of beauty because being the image of God—that which has the special privilege to embody and realize the glory of God—is the exact definition of beauty.

This theology of beauty and transformation assumes something about the nature of humanity that our culture is inclined to deny. Paul is saying that the way to be transformed into who you were meant to be, the way to become truly beautiful, is to look outside of yourself, not inside of yourself. It will not be gazing in the mirror that you find your beauty. It will be gazing upon your God. It will not be in positive self-talk and self-help books that you become the "you" you've always wanted to be. It will be through a fixed contemplation on who your God is. *Beauty is not about being independent. It is all about being dependent because beauty is essentially reflective.* And therefore, as long as we refuse to look upon the reality we were made to reflect, we will never be transformed.

As long as we object to being a walking, talking representation of our God, we will fail to be fully beautiful. As long as we assert our independence from God, we will fall short of true beauty. We will only reach true glory as our eyes feast upon our Lord and Savior. But if we only stare into the mirror, we deny that which makes us human and that which makes us beautiful: being *God's* image, not our own.

We can also conclude that transformation does not ultimately come by way of physical remedies. In a culture of anti-aging and cosmetic surgery, it is hard to believe that we actually think we are beautiful just as we are (even though that's what we are supposed to say). We talk a lot about being content with who we are while plastic surgery is getting increasingly more common. But the transformation we need will not come through lip fillers, serums, acne pills, or boob jobs. Ultimately, our transformation will come through reflecting on who God is. It is in "beholding the glory of the Lord" that we "are being transformed" (2 Corinthians 3:18). Not in beholding the glory of ourselves, but in beholding the glory of the Lord. That is what will actually transform us. If we are unsatisfied with what we see in the mirror, no cosmetic remedy will truly cure us. Even if it works, even if you have plump lips, radiant skin, and a perfect chest, that will not ultimately transform you into something truly beautiful. It is only by beholding God's glory that we begin the long process of transformation from that which is ugly and imperfect to that which is beautiful and perfected.

This wisdom from Paul offers comfort to those of us who will never be content with our earthly bodies. This is Paul's insight for those whom, no matter how hard they try, cannot believe they are beautiful: yes, your body now manifests the brokenness of the world around you, but as you fix your eyes upon your Savior, you are slowly being transformed to manifest the glory of his character that your body will one day indeed match. 2 Corinthians chapter 3 tells us that we are currently being transformed into glory, but yesterday we read in chapter 4 that this transformation is still one of inward glory rather than bodily glory, as long as we are on earth. And so we cannot expect to be fully satisfied with our physical appearance while on earth. But we take hope in Paul's words that as we behold God's glory, we are being transformed. This transformation today may only be spiritual, but in its consummation, it will include the physical. For in Philippians 3:20-21, Paul reminds us that "our citizenship is in heaven, and from it we await a Savior, the Lord Jesus Christ, who will transform our lowly body to be like his glorious body, by the power that enables him even to subject all things to himself." This tells us that the power at work within your heart transforming you spiritually at this moment, the power of the Lord Jesus Christ, is the very same power that will one day transform you physically. And so we wait, longing for the day in which our bodies reflect the glory of God. We wait by gazing at that very glory—contemplating our Master's grandeur, and in so doing, embodying it.

REFLECTION & APPLICATION:

1. *Have you gone a day without looking in the mirror? How does our culture's obsession with looking at ourselves contribute to our insecurities? Instead of looking in the mirror so much, what does Paul's teaching in this passage suggest will help?*

2. *When you struggle with your appearance, do you turn inward or outward? Paul wants us to look up when we are insecure, not to look in.*

3. *What are practical ways you can start "beholding the glory of the Lord"? Think about how art can powerfully communicate God's glory to us. What art forms could help you meditate on God's glory? What is the other main source of revelation for the Christian? How can that help us "behold" our God?*

RESURRECTION

What They

TELL YOU:

"You only live once!"

READ 1 CORINTHIANS 15

What God

TELLS YOU:

"And if Christ has not been raised, your faith is futile; you are still in your sins. Then those also who have fallen asleep in Christ are lost. If only for this life we have hope in Christ, we are of all people most to be pitied."

1 CORINTHIANS 15:17-19

I n 1 Corinthians 15, Paul ends his letter to this very messy church in Corinth with a reminder that they must cling to the original gospel he first preached to them: "that Christ died for our sins according to the Scriptures, that he was buried, that he was raised on the third day according to the Scriptures" (1 Corinthians 15:1-4). This gospel must be preserved at all costs. Indeed, false teaching wreaked havoc in Corinth because the people didn't properly conform to the gospel message. Apparently, some people in Corinth suggested there was no resurrection of the dead. Paul considered this false doctrine that directly contradicted the gospel: if people are not raised from the dead, then Christ was also not raised from the dead (1 Corinthians 15:13). And if Christ was not raised from the dead, the gospel is not true (1 Corinthians 15:14-15). Paul wants to be clear about the huge implications for such a belief as denying the resurrection. He goes as far as to say that if they accept this doctrine as true, then his preaching and their faith is *useless* (1 Corinthians 15:14). Why is the resurrection such a pivotal doctrine? Isn't the important part that Jesus died for our sins?

Paul claims that without the resurrection, our faith is worthless because we remain in our sins nonetheless (1 Corinthians 15:17). Why might this be? We normally think about the death of Christ when reassuring ourselves that we are forgiven of our sins. What could the resurrection have to do with such reassurance? Think of it this way: when Christ was condemned by the human court in Jerusalem, he received the punishment due for his supposed "crime," which was death. Conversely, when Christ was judged by the ultimate Judge, God himself in the heavenly courtroom, he received the reward due for his perfect life, which was resurrection. The human court declared Jesus guilty by killing him; the heavenly court declared Jesus innocent by raising him. The resurrection is God's stamp of approval on Christ's atoning work on the cross. Jesus was not just another false Messiah. By raising Christ from the dead, God declares that Jesus' death was no normal death. In Romans 4:25 Paul says that Christ was "delivered up for our trespasses and raised for our justification." So Paul here is associating Christ's death with the punishment of sin (being delivered up for our trespasses) and the resurrection with God's acceptance of the atonement of Christ (being raised for our justification). Because God has accepted the sacrificial offering of Christ's blood for our sins, we can be justified. The New Testament writers see the resurrection as God's grand vindication and acceptance of the work of the Son. If Jesus died and that was the end of the story, we have no reason to believe he was the Son of God and the ultimate sacrifice for our sins. But in the resurrection, God puts his stamp of approval upon Jesus, and therefore, upon us, too. Without the resurrection, we are not fully justified; we are still "in our sins" (1 Corinthians 15:17).

Therefore, Paul condemns the teaching that ignores the resurrection of Christ because it distorts a central part of the gospel message; in fact, it renders the gospel completely ineffective. Indeed, Paul says if this anti-resurrection doctrine is true, then Christians ought to be a pitied people group (I Corinthians 15:19). Others should feel bad for us! We are the people who only have "hope" in this life, and therefore, we deserve the sympathies of those around us. If there is no life after death, Christians are just left with what this life has to offer. Without belief in the resurrection, says Paul, Christians ought to be belittled because they have no real hope.

It seems that sometimes the contemporary church has also lost concern for the importance of the resurrection. While many Christians do not deny a resurrection of the saints, it is certainly not a prominent part of their theology. In the West, we live lives that are more distant from death than any other culture, historically speaking. That is why the year of the COVID-19 pandemic was an "unprecedented year." We are not used to facing death so often and so closely. Our lives are rarely spent in fear of death. Some of us go decades without even losing a person close to us. For many Americans, death does not confront us daily. But for the large majority of human history, death felt much closer to the human experience. Infants often died young. People did not have life expectancies into their 80s. They did not have modern medicine to fight disease. They did not have modern technology to secure the resources they needed. But today, in our technological and scientific age, we approach the world with a completely different attitude. The world is not handed to us as it is. We do not have to conform to its ways; rather, we see the world as malleable. We assume that the world can be conformed to our ways. And so we do not hope and pray for a good harvest season and mourn when the land does not grant it to us as the ancients did. Rather, we build technology that ensures each season will be like the last. While the ancients and many generations after them saw the world as full of inevitabilities (things beyond their control), the modern self looks on the world as being "without form and void." As if we can bring order out of the chaos as the word of God does in Genesis 1. We think we can make it into whatever we wish it to be.

And when we are so absorbed in a world of possibility rather than inevitability, death can seem less threatening. We are not forced to stare death in the face very often. Physical suffering, in general, is more easily avoided in the modern West. We do not have to do many hard things ourselves anymore because we have machines that do it for us. Technology has made a life of ease for mankind in the West. This has the tendency to disconnect us from the historical experience of the world in which suffering was inevitable and common. Death could not be ignored. A year of sickness, death, wars, and chaos was not thought to be unprecedented. In fact, it probably seemed quite normal. And so, our comfy lives on planet earth mean that our theology of death is less urgent. Life can be pretty nice sometimes; we aren't always dying to get to the other side. And on top of that, death isn't coming for us anytime soon. We assume that we have a solid 70-80 years to figure all that depressing stuff out. This means that it is less important to many of us how different religious systems deal with death because death seems like a far away reality. But if the past few years of American history have reminded us of anything, it is that we are not in control of life, and death is always waiting at our doorstep. In a biblical framework, there is a sense that we are all dangling on the brink of death, not just the people in the ICU. We are all like grass. Mankind "flourishes like a flower of the field; for the wind passes over it, and it is gone, and its place knows it no more" (Psalm 103:15-16). Each day is yet another day in which we might return to the dust from which we were made.

Under this biblical view of death, a view that takes death seriously, the resurrection of Christ is the crown of Christian theology. It is the hope that out of death can come life again, even life unstained by sin. Only the Christian religion deals with the reality of death in such a glorious way. Therefore, the Christian who wants to understand the true nature of biblical hope must first understand the inevitability of death and the certain hope of resurrection. The popular use of the term "YOLO" is quite ironic in a society that doesn't take the reality of death seriously. We use the phrase as permission to go all out and take chances in life, but we seem to forget the depressing reality that such a statement includes: you only live once, and when you die, it's over. Completely over. But Christians today must fight this notion, clinging to the doctrine of the resurrection as the pinnacle statement of Christianity. We must meditate on its truth and protect it from neglect as the apostle Paul did. We do not want to be a people with a hope in this life only, as most are in our country today. We are not a people to be pitied. We are a people who have attained that which the nations long for: hope of life after death. We must never stop gazing at the future, for we will lose the essence of Christianity when we separate it from the reality of our coming resurrection.

Therefore, resurrection plays a key role in the Christian identity. First, it reminds us that death does not have the final say on who we are, just like it did not have the final say on who Jesus was. Second, it reminds us that God will not throw away our physical nature but renew it in eternity. Paul puts it this way later on in chapter 15: "So is it with the resurrection of the dead. What is sown is perishable; what is raised is imperishable. It is sown in dishonor; it is raised in glory. It is sown in weakness; it is raised in power. It is sown a natural body; it is raised a spiritual body" (1 Corinthians 15:42-44). Our resurrected bodies will be clothed in a glory that far surpasses the glory of our current body. So Paul's response to your body-image problems is not, "Who cares?! Physical stuff doesn't matter anyway. It's all about being spiritual. Your physical body will be nothing one day!" Rather Paul essentially says to our insecure selves, "The body you now inhabit will one day be restored to utter perfection, and you will no longer need to hide in fear of exposure. Your body will not disintegrate into nothingness; it will be transformed into an everlasting body. Your body is sacred. Your total salvation includes your body. It needs saving, too." What a powerful message is the physical, bodily resurrection in a day and age where women are continually oppressed by feelings of body shame. Christianity does not ignore this pervasive feeling of physical inadequacy. It offers the ultimate remedy. Take heart, ladies: God will raise your imperfect bodies to perfect ones. And it will be awesome. You are not a woman to be pitied, for you have a hope that goes beyond this life.

REFLECTION & APPLICATION:

1. *How has our technologically advanced society compromised our sense of inevitability in the world? Why is this a bad thing, especially when we think about death? Why do we need to recognize the inevitability of death?*

2. *Why is the resurrection such a pivotal doctrine in Paul's mind? Why is it still relevant for us today?*

3. *How does our belief in resurrection affect our Christian identity? How does it specifically speak to the problem of body-image? Does the Christian have a low view of the body and only care about the spiritual part of existence?*

Corporate

SELF

What They

TELL YOU:

"Faith is all about finding yourself."

READ EPHESIANS 4

What God

TELLS YOU:

"And he gave the apostles, the prophets, the evangelists, the shepherds and teachers, to equip the saints for the work of ministry, for building up the body of Christ, until we all attain to the unity of the faith and of the knowledge of the Son of God, to mature manhood, to the measure of the stature of the fullness of Christ."

EPHESIANS 4:11-13

P aul begins Ephesians chapter 4 with a call to live a life "worthy of the calling" of Christ (Ephesians 4:1). This means a life of humility, gentleness, patience, and love. It also means to live a life with an eagerness to "maintain the unity of the Spirit" (Ephesians 4:3). What might this mean? Paul elaborates on what he means by this in verses 4-16 by reflecting on the nature of the church. Every member of the church is filled by one Spirit, unified thereby to one body, called to one hope, one Lord, one faith, one baptism, and of course, one God (Ephesians 4:4-6). This list of unifying characteristics creates a *corporate identity* for the church.

Each individual has so much in common with her fellow believers that they take on a singular identity. But this corporate identity does not wipe out our individuality and personal giftings. Indeed, God's grace is extended to each individual through Christ, granting each her own specific gifts. These gifts create distinct identities within the body of Christ (Ephesians 4:7). There are leaders within the church—Paul lists the apostles, the prophets, the evangelists, the shepherds and teachers (Ephesians 4:11)—all of which are mandated to equip the rest of the church for other specific roles of ministry. All the saints work together for the purpose of "building up the body of Christ" (Ephesians 4:12). In this way, *each saint commits themselves to an individual calling for the sake of the corporate calling.* Each believer functions in their distinct role in the context of the entire body. And ultimately, the task of the church becomes a corporate task, not an individual one. The church, as one body, builds itself up until the day when "we all attain to the unity of the faith and of the knowledge of the Son of God, to mature manhood, to the measure of the stature of the fullness of the Son of God" (Ephesians 4:13). This is the task of the *many* ("we all") with the goal of becoming *one*—the Greek of "mature manhood" is literally "a full-grown man" in the singular. Therefore, though we are each called individually, our goal of becoming one dominates our identity and purpose.

Paul continues this metaphor of a "full grown man" by saying that the goal of the church is to "grow up in every way into him who is the head, into Christ, from whom the whole body, joined and held together by every joint with which it is equipped, when each part is working properly, makes the body grow so that it builds itself up in love" (Ephesians 4:15-16). By using the metaphor of a body and head, Paul is creating a corporate identity for the church. They are not to think of themselves in isolation. *Their sense of self is to be dominated by their corporate identity.* Not only is their identity dominated by their union with Christ, but it is also dominated by their union with all the other people unified to Christ. Believers become one with Christ and one with each other. Therefore, they are always to think of themselves as a part of a whole. Christians are not individual, independent beings. We are inevitably and intimately connected with all who call on the name of Jesus. If one person has the individual identity as a "hand," they can only identify as so by acknowledging that a hand makes up a part of a body with legs, arms, feet, and a head. Our individual identity is only understood in the context of our corporate identity. We can only be a "hand" if we are indeed part of a "body." Paul suggests that if each part is functioning properly, it will lead to further intimacy within the body. In fact, this text suggests that the *telos* of the church— the ultimate end or destiny of the church—is oneness. The church will reach ultimate authenticity when they become one body, under the head of Christ. This means that when we properly understand our identity (as a part of a whole), it will lead to further connection within the church and will more closely knit us together as the body of Christ.

This passage is typically used today to highlight how God gives each believer a unique set of gifts and skills to impact the world. It may be our modern ears that hear a text like this and immediately begin to think about individuality in the church. Our minds are tuned towards individual expression and celebration. We tend to think that the peak of authentic human life is when we can each fully express our individuality. As a result, we impose such assumptions on the biblical text and assume God has the same goal in mind for the church. The church becomes a place for people to perform and express who they want to be because this is what we envision as true humanity. But the metaphor of the church as the body of Christ, though it does speak to our diverse individual roles, is ultimately a metaphor that declares the unity of the church. It is more about our oneness than it is about our differences. *It is more about our corporate identity than it is about our individual identity. And it is more about us conforming than it is about us performing.*

Let me clarify. Our individualistic culture wants to make society and communities places that ultimately serve the individual. So in individualistic societies, communities become places where individuals can "perform." This does not mean they can get up on a stage and do a dance for everyone, but it does mean they see society and community as the place where they are to express themselves and be recognized for such expression. But the corporate vision of community (found in Ephesians 4) is one in which the individuals serve the group; the group does not serve the individuals. This does not mean individuals lose all that makes them distinct from one another, but it means *individuality ought to be used for the good of the whole, not for individual recognition.* In this sense, individuals enter into the church community to be conformed. But this kind of conformity is not oppressive nor repressive. It is actually the way we become who we were meant to be. We are conformed into the body, becoming one with fellow believers. And in so doing we are conformed into the likeness of Christ, our corporate head and the ultimate image of God. We do not participate in the covenant community merely to express our individuality; we participate in the covenant community to become partakers in the divine nature of Christ.

While this may seem nit-picky, this is a serious problem the church is facing today. If we refuse to acknowledge the biblical priority of our corporate identity and exalt the individual over the group, we lose the mission of the church because the mission of the church is essentially corporate. Our future is not an individual future. Our task is not an individual task. Our goal is not an individual goal. Christian identity cannot be understood apart from the church. The call of discipleship is fundamentally a group calling. We cannot do it alone. And as long as we make church a place where we are supposed to be recognized, celebrated, and where we can live out our individuality as we please, we will fail to attain the "unity of faith" and become the "full-grown man." If we insist on making church about expressing ourselves instead of serving other selves, we will fail to be a church at all. Each part is working properly when it has a vision of its purpose for the whole. *We* are to grow up in our head. Not *me*. But *we*. So if we want to understand our future identity in Christ, we have to understand that it's not about "me," it's about "we."

REFLECTION **&** APPLICATION:

1. *Why is church attendance a key part of identity reinforcement for the Christian? Do you have consistent participation in a church community? Remember, discipleship cannot be done alone. What are some ways you could focus on the "we" of discipleship instead of the "me" of discipleship?*

2. *Can you think of any ways that you make church a place for your "performance" and self-expression rather than a place of worship and fellowship?*

3. *How can you use your individuality to serve the common goal of the church rather than to satisfy your own desires?*

Worshiping

SELF

What They

TELL YOU:

"Finding yourself is all about learning to celebrate yourself."

READ REVELATION 7

What God

TELLS YOU:

"After this I looked, and behold, a great multitude that no one could number, from every nation, from all tribes and peoples and languages, standing before the throne and before the Lamb, clothed in white robes, with palm branches in their hands, and crying out with a loud voice, 'Salvation belongs to our God who sits on the throne, and to the Lamb!' And all the angels were standing around the throne and around the elders and the four living creatures, and they fell on their faces before the throne and worshiped God, saying, 'Amen! Blessing and glory and wisdom and thanksgiving and honor and power and might be to our God forever and ever! Amen.'"

REVELATION 7:9-12

I t seems only appropriate that as we reflect on the "Future Self" we meditate on the book of Revelation. We certainly do not have the space here to discuss the many diverse ways of understanding the book of Revelation. Thankfully, the different interpretative frameworks for the book do not affect the basic meaning of our particular passage very much. The message is fairly clear no matter how you interpret the book as a whole. As John continues in his visions of glory, he encounters a "great multitude that no one could number, from every nation" (Revelation 7:9). This mob stands before the throne of God, clothed in white robes, waving palm branches. They cry out that "Salvation belongs to our God" (Revelation 7:10). And not only they, but even the angels fall on their faces in worship, declaring "Amen! Blessing and glory and wisdom and thanksgiving and honor and power and might be to our God forever and ever! Amen" (Revelation 7:12). A man, apparently an "elder," approaches John asking who these people are, but John claims that he already knows (Revelation 7:14). Indeed the elder responds proclaiming that "These are the ones coming out of the great tribulation. They have washed their robes and made them white in the blood of the Lamb" (Revelation 7:14).

What exactly "the great tribulation" refers to will differ depending on a reader's overall interpretation of Revelation, but what is clear is that this group of people are the redeemed people of God, for they are the people who have been washed by the blood of the Lamb and clothed in his righteousness. Indeed they are those who "are before the throne of God" and those who "serve him day and night in his temple" (Revelation 7:15). As if establishing a new priesthood, the people of God spend eternity serving in worship of Yahweh. And this worship is not without its benefits, for "he who sits on the throne will shelter them with his presence. They shall hunger no more, neither thirst anymore; the sun shall not strike them, nor any scorching heat. For the Lamb in the midst of the throne will be their shepherd, and he will guide them to springs of living water, and God will wipe away every tear from their eyes" (Revelation 7:15-17). No one can doubt that this vision represents the perfection of eternity, where those who have believed in Christ will worship and enjoy God forever.

This passage offers us an important consideration when we think of our future self. Just as we consider the *telos* of the church is to become one in Christ (Ephesians 4), so too we must consider the *telos* of the church as eternal worshipers. This passage is the culmination of the biblical theme of worship and temple. In fairly recent biblical scholarship, academics have noticed that the garden of Eden constitutes many features that parallel that of the temple. The Garden

was the place where God "walked" among mankind (Genesis 3:8), just
as God "walked" in his temple (Leviticus 26:11-12). God and man
dwelled together in Eden. But due to the fall, mankind was banished
east of the Garden, separated from their life source and their loving
God. From there, God places a cherubim, creatures that represent
divine throne-bearers and guards, in front of the east gate of the
Garden (Genesis 3:24). The presence of God is now guarded by a
gate and by cherubim from his people. What is interesting is that the
temple, which is striving to restore Eden by allowing God to dwell
among man, was built hundreds of years after this horrible incident
in the Garden but would mimic this very structure. As the place where
God dwells, the main temple gate was located on the east, just as the
Garden was entered through the east. The Holy of Holies within the
temple was guarded by cherubim on the altar, just as the cherubim
guarded the presence of God after banishing Adam and Eve. It is as if
the temple rebuilds a mini Eden amidst the people of Israel.

Also interesting is that the description of the priests during the time
of the temple is the same basic job description originally given to
Adam and Eve in the Garden: "to work and keep." "To work," in
Hebrew is also often translated as "to serve." It can refer to physical
labor, but also religious devotion or service; therefore, it is also often
translated as "worship" or "minister." Likewise, "to keep" is a very
rich word in Hebrew. It can be translated as "to watch," "to preserve,"
"to guard,"and even "to obey." It is this word that is used when
referring to "keeping" God's covenant or his commandments. The
first couple's job description to work and keep was not just merely an

agricultural task. It was a larger call to worship, serve, and obey God as stewards of his creation, as people living in his presence. And, in Numbers 3:7-8, the priests are given the same job description for their work in the temple. They are to "minister" (work) and to "keep guard" (keep); these are the same exact verbs commanded to Adam and Eve in Genesis 2. It seems this is because the temple recreates the garden of Eden, where mankind can resume their role as priests within God's order.

What is most important for our discussion of our future self is that this original human identity as a priest in the garden of God seems to be restored here in Revelation. Just as Adam and Eve served God in the Garden, the redeemed people "are before the throne of God and serve him day and night in his temple" (Revelation 7:15). This Greek term for "serve" is related to the Hebrew word for serve in that it also often refers to worship. When Jesus is tempted by Satan in the wilderness, he responds by quoting the Scriptures, saying: "You shall *worship* the Lord your God and him only shall you *serve*" (Matthew 4:10). To worship and to serve are parallel ideas. By saying that the people in robes in Revelation *serve* God day and night, John is saying they *worship* God day and night. Indeed, the original sanctuary of Eden is finally restored in the book of Revelation. Humanity is able to take up their role as priests before their God once again. And this means that from Genesis to Revelation, God is working to restore human beings to their original purpose: worshipers. The role of the Old Testament priest was to serve God in his temple; it was a partial restoration of the garden of Eden. But it came with many obstacles because of God's holiness and our sinfulness. But now that Christ has taken care of our sin by washing our robes and making them white in the blood of the Lamb (Revelation 7:14), we can serve God as priests with no need of bloody sacrifice and no fear of death.

This overarching theme throughout the Bible teaches us important things about biblical identity. As we have mentioned before, our identity is determined by our purpose. If Adam and Eve's purpose was to be priests in the sanctuary of God, then they would only be their most authentic selves when they could do so without restraint. And that is why, after Jesus' death, the curtain in the temple being torn in two is such a climactic moment (Matthew 27:51). The death of Christ, as the ultimate sacrifice for sins, makes a way for us to re-enter the temple as priests of God. We can draw near to our God once again. We can serve him and dwell among him as we were always meant to. The torn veil is a representation that the work of Christ will eventually lead to complete, free access to our God and Father. We will finally be able to do what we were made to do: worship.

The book of Revelation completes the story that began all the way back in Genesis 1. It is the story of humanity forfeiting its true identity for a false one, but having that true identity restored once and for all by the gracious love of their Savior and God. And though today they do not serve their Master face to face, they look forward to the day of their self-realization. Unlike the popular imagination, the day of self-realization is not the day of complete independence and self-fulfillment. The day of self-realization is the day in which they can freely worship God forever. It is only in that day "They shall hunger no more, neither thirst anymore; the sun shall not strike them, nor any scorching heat. For the Lamb in the midst of the throne will be their shepherd, and he will guide them to springs of living water, and God will wipe away every tear from their eyes" (Revelation 7:16-17). All of the darkness and pain we know so intimately here on earth will be finally taken away when we are able to fully embrace our identity as worshipers in eternity. Do you know your destiny, child of God? Do you know your purpose? You are destined to be a priest. A priest who has the privilege to serve their God in perfect peace and joy into infinity. And the Good News is that this self-realization is not dependent on you working hard enough; it is dependent on the blood of Christ. Your true self will be realized. You have nothing to fear.

REFLECTION **&** APPLICATION:

1. *How are Adam and Eve "priests" in the garden of Eden? What does that tell us about their identity? What does it tell us about our original purpose as human beings?*

2. *A lot of people use the term "self-realization" to refer to "finding themselves." But for the Christian, what does self-realization look like? How and when do we achieve ultimate authenticity in our identity? Is it by finding ourselves or by God finding us?*

3. *What is your destiny as a believer in Christ? How should that affect your daily living?*

Hopeful
SELF

What They

TELL YOU:

"Hope is all about having faith in yourself. You make your own destiny."

READ JUDE

What God

TELLS YOU:

"Now to him who is able to keep you from stumbling and to present you blameless before the presence of his glory with great joy, to the only God, our Savior, through Jesus Christ our Lord, be glory, majesty, dominion, and authority, before all time and now and forever. Amen."

JUDE 24-25

The book of Jude may be easily forgotten or even neglected, due to its miniature size or, more likely, because of its especially fiery content. Jude, a servant of Jesus Christ and brother of James, has no hesitation in saying what needs to be said. While he certainly would have preferred a letter of butterflies and rainbows, he was compelled to share a tougher message: "Beloved, although I was very eager to write to you about our common salvation, I found it necessary to write appealing to you to contend for the faith that was once for all delivered to the saints" (Jude 3). While Jude mentions no specific church as the recipient of his letter, whichever community to whom this was delivered was clearly being seduced by false teachers "who pervert the grace of our God into sensuality and deny our only Master and Lord, Jesus Christ" (Jude 4). Jude gives this church the important reminder that distortion of the gospel will ultimately lead to destruction. And he does not hold back from speaking openly and boldly about judgment. Jude is prepared to give a hard word when it is needed. But by the end of the letter, Jude seeks to comfort the church. He will not let his last words be harsh in their current struggle. He encourages them saying, "But you must remember, beloved, the predictions of the apostles of our Lord Jesus Christ. They said to you, 'In the last time there will be scoffers, following their own ungodly passions'" (Jude 17-18). Jude is saying that we have been warned. The apostles predicted these tough times. Jesus knew this would happen. God's plan has not taken a turn for the worst. Despite the scoffers, the people of God are to continue building themselves up in their faith, praying in the Holy Spirit, keeping themselves in the love of God, and waiting for his mercies to come (Jude 20-21).

This all culminates in his final doxology that serves to remind the church of their hope: "Now to him who is able to keep you from stumbling and to present you blameless before the presence of his glory with great joy, to the only God, our Savior, through Jesus Christ our Lord, be glory, majesty, dominion, and authority, before all time and now and forever. Amen" (Jude 24-25). Why does the church have hope in the midst of such brokenness and sin? They have hope because it is not they that will sustain themselves to the end, it is he. *He* is the one who is able to keep us from stumbling. Not only that, but *he* is the one able to present us "blameless" before the glory of God. Blameless! What we can see in this text is that the Christian virtue of hope is completely dependent on the nature of God. They can have hope because they believe in a God "who is able."

Therefore, faith and hope are inevitably intertwined. The Christian can only have as much hope as they have faith in the person in whom their hope depends on. In other words, if you do not have faith that

God is who he says he is, then you won't have hope that he will do what he says he will do. Paul, in Romans 4, speaks of this connection when considering Abraham and the promise of a child despite his old age and his barren wife. Paul says that *"in hope he believed"* (Romans 4:18). What does hope have to do with belief? Paul goes on, "No unbelief made him waver concerning the promise of God, but he grew strong in his faith as he gave glory to God, *fully convinced that God was able to do what he had promised"* (Romans 4:20-21). Abraham was able to grow strong in faith and to not waver in unbelief because he was fully convinced that God would do what he said he would do. He believed in an all-powerful and all-faithful God; therefore, he had hope that God's promises would certainly come about. Christian hope is based on Christian theology: the nature of God. It is only because God is the unchanging and always reliable Creator of all things that Abraham has hope in this otherwise extremely unlikely promise. His faith in the God of the Bible is the basis for his certainty in the promise (hope). Faith and hope go hand in hand.

And so it is in the book of Jude. The hope of the church is based on who they know their God to be: "him who is able to keep you from stumbling and to present you blameless before the presence of his glory" (Jude 24). Just as he is the one who was able to grant a barren woman conception, he is also the one who is able to keep us from stumbling and present us blameless before his presence (even as that seems just as impossible as a barren woman conceiving at over 100 years old!). When we understand biblical hope as something dependent on belief in the biblical God, we begin to see how culture has lost any true sense of the virtue of hope. Culture wants to keep the confident expectations that hope offers; they want to keep the positive outlooks that hope encourages. But they are also prone to eliminate the belief in the God who provides such hope. Therefore, hope often has no real grounding in our culture.

Rather, faith and hope are usually used in the secular realm merely to indicate wishful thinking. It is the vague sense that "everything is going to be alright." It may sometimes include a "gut-feeling" that God is on our side, though *why* we might think that is rarely explained. But other times, hope is completely isolated from belief in a certain kind of God and instead is purely based on self-confidence. Hope just becomes another way of expressing faith in oneself. But that sentence is one that would only make sense in modern ears. Historically, faith has been a trust in something outside of yourself. Having faith never referred to the self. But now, we often use faith as an expression of self-assurance. "Have faith in yourself!" they tell you. "Never underestimate yourself! Never doubt that you can accomplish anything you set your mind to!" People today would call these statements of faith. But biblically (and historically), they hardly fit the category. Faith has nothing to do with self-confidence. That is more regularly identified as foolishness in the Scriptures. *Faith is confidence in something other than yourself.* Our secular understanding of faith would be awfully puzzling to the biblical authors and most Christians throughout history. Because we have warped our understanding of faith to be about ourselves instead of God, we have distorted hope to be something found within ourselves. *Just as biblical hope is dependent on faith in who God is, secular hope is dependent on faith in who you are.* This is a prime example of how our culture teaches us to orient everything towards the self. We have taken distinctly religious virtues such as faith and hope and managed to make them about ourselves.

Just as in the case of faith, hope has also become a form of self-assurance. When people say they have "hope" today, they likely are saying they have confidence that *they are able* to get the job done. But in the Scriptures, hope is the confidence that *God is able* to get the job done, just as we have seen in Jude and Romans. Realizing this distinction, we can come to understand what a biblical theology of hope has to do with our sense of self. How does hope relate to our Christian identity? It all goes back to whether we see ourselves as essentially independent, autonomous beings or whether we see ourselves as essentially dependent, subordinate beings. While the latter option likely sounds less appealing, we must fight to see the beauty of it in practice. We are not sovereign. We are not in control. We are not able to ensure certain ends. Only God is. This ought to let the Christian breathe a sigh of relief. This is not on you. Faith is not belief in yourself. It is belief in God. Hope is not confidence in yourself. It is confidence in God.

We love the idea of being independent, self-reliant people until we are forced to face the reality that we have no control over so many factors in life. Jude saw a lot of threats to the church of his day. I am sure he also faced plenty of individual threats, but he can end his letter in joy and triumph because of his biblical understanding of hope. He is able to be sure of victory because he knows that the battle belongs to the Lord. Let us beware that the modern view of the self has compromised one of the most comforting biblical doctrines: hope is not about you, it's about God. Lift your eyes to the hills. Where does your help come from? Your help comes from the Lord, who made heaven and earth (Psalm 121:1-2). It does not come from yourself. Self-help does not understand biblical hope. Therefore, an identity built upon self-help cannot enjoy the certainty of the promises of triumph that biblical hope provides. When you cannot help yourself, God can. The hopeful self is the self that is confident first in who God is, not first in who we are. The hopeful self is the self who can say in full assurance that God is the one who "is able to keep you from stumbling and to present you blameless before the presence of his glory with great joy!" (Jude 24). And that's good news.

REFLECTION & APPLICATION:

1.   *What is the biblical connection between faith and hope? How does what we believe inform what we hope for? What is the biblical conception of confidence?*

2.   *What do people today often mean when they say they "have faith" or "have hope"? How is that different from the biblical understanding? Why does it matter?*

3.   *Why is faith and hope in ourselves inadequate? Why do we need faith in something greater than ourselves? How is the biblical doctrine of hope comforting?*

WEEK SIX

Not

YOURSELF

The Purpose of

SALVATION

What They

TELL YOU:

"When you say 'yes' to others, make sure you are not saying 'no' to yourself."

READ 2 CORINTHIANS 5

What God

TELLS YOU:

"For the love of Christ controls us, because we have concluded this: that one has died for all, therefore all have died; and he died for all, that those who live might no longer live for themselves but for him who for their sake died and was raised."

2 CORINTHIANS 5:14–15

As we finish our journey through a biblical theology of identity and self-image, we end with a reminder of the correct emphasis in this entire discussion. Though we have toiled to see what the Bible says about self-esteem and self-understanding, we must realize that its greatest focus is not on the self. It is on others. Its emphasis is on our need to esteem and understand others, not the need to esteem and understand the self. In fact, it seems that when we learn to esteem God and esteem others, we achieve the healthy self-esteem we have always wanted. It would be a deadly mistake to finish a devotional on biblical selfhood without reminding ourselves that it really isn't all about ourselves. As we have spent our time reflecting on the perceived self, the broken self, the redeemed self, the physical self, and the future self, we will end with a meditation appropriately titled, "Not Yourself."

We have seen multiple times throughout our study how Paul defends his apostleship before the trouble-making Corinthian church, and we have seen how his understanding of identity has played a key role in that process. In 2 Corinthians 4, Paul describes the suffering he endures as an apostle of Christ. But he will not lose heart because he knows that his worldly appearance is not indicative of the glorious work he does. He reminds the Corinthians that "though our outer self is wasting away, our inner self is being renewed day by day" (2 Corinthians 4:16). Paul is not concerned with appearances when he knows the reality. It may look like he is falling to pieces, but, in truth, he is being made whole! He chooses to not fixate on that which is seen but to look to that which is unseen, which is eternal (2 Corinthians 4:18).

However, it becomes clear in chapter 5 that the Corinthians church is unconvinced of his argument that appearance is not always indicative of reality. Paul receives pushback from them on his leadership due to the fact that he lives a less-than-glamorous life, often being persecuted and humiliated. The Corinthian church feels that it is unfit for a leader of the church to live such a life of shame. Paul was not being very "seeker-sensitive" having this kind of reputation. He made the church look pathetic and weak. No one wants to come and find out how to be the scum of the earth! How are they going to get people in the doors? Paul was bad for business. This becomes clear in verses 12 and 13 when Paul says, "We are not commending ourselves to you again but giving you cause to boast about us, so that you may be able to answer those who boast about outward appearance and not about what is in the heart. For if we are beside ourselves, it is for God; if we are in our right mind, it is for you" (2 Corinthians 5:12-13). When Paul says he is not trying to "commend" himself to them again, he is saying that he is not trying to make himself look good and get people's approval and applause, but rather he wants the Corinthians to be confident in his leadership and to trust him. The word "boast" in Greek is connected with the notion of confidence and assurance. When he says he wants to give the church a reason to boast about him, he is saying he wants them to be confident in his faithful, trustworthy leadership.

This is so that they can defend their church leaders when opposed by those who have a flashy, noble outward appearance but a spoiled heart. These leaders "boast about outward appearance" rather than integrity, but their outward appearance is just a mask for a sinful heart. Paul wants them to understand that if he appears humiliated or "beside himself," it is for God's sake and theirs. It is not because he is a pathetic weakling. Rather, it is because the gospel controls his mind. This is where we find the beautiful words of verse 14 and 15: "For the love of Christ controls us, because we have concluded this: that one has died for all, therefore all have died; and he died for all, that those who live might no longer live for themselves but for him who for their sake died and was raised." The love of Christ causes Paul to live a life of hardship and even degradation. Paul's life is completely oriented towards the service of Christ and his neighbor. And if the people of Corinth find that belittling or unprofessional, then it is the gospel that they deny, not just Paul's leadership.

Verses 15-17 operate as a sort of conclusion to Paul's long response to the church's concerns about appearing cowardly. He is saying that this is the essence of the gospel: a life of service. Who was Jesus? One man who was willing to be humiliated for the sake of another. One man who suffers so that another might not have to. One man who looked like a coward, but, in reality, was the strongest man alive. Jesus Christ did not live for himself. His entire life was a mission for the other.

The purpose of our salvation is that we might do the same. Just as he lived and died for another, we are to live and die for another. The purpose statement inside these verses is easy to miss in the text, so look closely. After proclaiming the truth of Jesus' others-oriented life and death, Paul uses the word "*that*" in verse 15: "and he died for all, *that...*" It is the equivalent to saying "so that." The "that" is a purpose clause. What comes after this crucial word is the reason behind Jesus' life, death, and resurrection. *Why* did Jesus live and die for all? "*That* those who live might no longer live for themselves but for him who for their sake died and was raised." The mission of salvation is to inspire selfless living; living that is no longer for the sake of the self, but for the other. And if that means looking bad, being mocked, suffering, or humiliation, so be it. That is what it meant for Christ as well. Paul's mind is so completely dominated by the love of Christ that he cannot help but live in a similar manner. The Corinthians thought it was demeaning to live a life like Paul's (and, they must have forgotten, like Christ's!), but, in reality, it was empowering because Paul was living into the purpose of his salvation—living not for himself, but for others.

Paul's vision of the purpose of the gospel contradicts much of the nuanced distortions that are popular today. Especially when preached to young women, the gospel has become a sort of self-esteem message. The gospel is the way in which you recieve the affirmation which you long for from others. The gospel's declaration that God loves you becomes synonymous with saying, "God thinks you're great." You might scroll through Christian instagram accounts and find aesthetic posts that say: "You are enough," "You are beautiful," "You are worthy." These kinds of phrases—and all the emphasis upon them— makes the gospel ultimately about self-love. The purpose of the gospel becomes about making you feel good about yourself. Jesus becomes your personal therapist and cheerleader in one. He is there to remind you to love yourself because he loves you. And often, many Christian women buy the self-love gospel without even thinking much about it. After all, it sounds so appealing.

Paul's gospel is quite simply the opposite. Jesus does not say celebrate yourself because he loves you. He says serve others because he loves them. It is not a gospel of self-love. It is a gospel of self-denial. He died so that we might learn to live for others. But many today, without even realizing it, have made the gospel about serving the self. We have let the insidious assumptions and trends of our day permeate our theology. And while the Christian gospel is a gospel of love, it is not really a gospel of self-love (at the very least, this is not the emphasis). This is an important distinction. It is a distinction that if we fail to recognize, we might end up buying a false gospel and never getting what we actually need. We might get a self-esteem boost. But we won't get atonement. And sadly, your self-esteem won't be any good to help you on the day of judgment, but atonement certainly will.

If we want to tap into the mind of Paul, we need a mind captivated by the self-sacrificial love of Christ. We need to be mesmerized by a love willing to lose so that another might win. We need to be enamoured by the power of humility. Only with this will we begin to want to walk in the treacherous footsteps of our Savior. Only then can we start to get excited about being the scum of the earth. And only then can we conceive of a selfless life as a good life. And so be mindful of gospel messages out there that seem to be more concerned with your self-esteem than your service.

We have seen that the Bible has plenty of rich wisdom when it comes to thinking about ourselves, but we have also seen that the center and purpose of the gospel is others-oriented, not self-oriented. Are you convinced that "one has died for all, therefore all have died; and he died for all, that those who live might no longer live for themselves but for him who for their sake died and was raised"? Then live like it.

REFLECTION & APPLICATION:

1. *When Paul says he is not looking for the "commendation" of others, it means he is not looking for their approval or applause. Where are you hungry for approval by others in your life? Instead of looking for praise, we should follow Paul's example and give people a reason to "boast" in us. Remember, to "boast" in this context is not the same as making much of someone. It refers to confidence in someone's reliability. Paul wants the church to be certain that he is dependable. How can you shift from looking for praise to striving for dependability?*

2. *What does Paul say is the purpose of Jesus' life, death, and resurrection? In our verse for today, what is the specific reason given for why Jesus died for us?*

3. *How does the self-love gospel distort the message of these verses? How does it miss the main point of the gospel? Do you ever make the gospel all about affirming yourself? Remember, God does not always affirm you, but he does always love you.*

Received

IDENTITY

"You determine who you are and what you will become."

READ ROMANS 6

What God

TELLS YOU:

"How can we who died to sin still live in it? Do you not know that all of us who have been baptized into Christ Jesus were baptized into his death? We were buried therefore with him by baptism into death, in order that, just as Christ was raised from the dead by the glory of the Father, we too might walk in newness of life... So you also must consider yourselves dead to sin and alive to God in Christ Jesus."

ROMANS 6:2-4,11

You may have heard the first eight chapters of Paul's letter to the Romans called "The Romans Road." This catchy name is quite fitting for this work of Paul's, for it takes us step by step through all the necessary parts of the gospel: from God's authority, to our sin and impending punishment, to the atoning life and death of Christ, and onto the lifestyle that proceeds from that reality. Today we consider chapter 6, which takes a crucial turn along the Romans Road. It moves on from theology into practice. In chapters 1 through 5, Paul carefully labors over the fundamental doctrines of the gospel. His writing has been largely educational rather than functional. He is determined to lay the proper theological foundation before he expounds the basics of Christian living in the rest of the letter. Chapter 6 makes it abundantly clear that Paul's theology and practice are intimately intertwined. He cannot sustain one without the other. Paul's practical instruction for everyday living comes right out of his understanding of the gospel. Paul moves from information to application so swiftly that we barely realize it.

As he tops off the theology portion of chapter 5 with the grand declaration that "where sin increased, grace abounded all the more" (Romans 5:20), he is left with an important question to kick off chapter 6: "What shall we say then? Are we to continue in sin that grace may abound?" (Romans 6:1). Paul anticipates people will take this Good News of God's infinite forgiveness to mean they can happily continue in sin. After all, our sin just lets God show off his grace, right? "By no means!" says Paul. He wants to make sure people don't mistake God's grace as a license to keep on sinning. He shows us this by explaining the gospel one more time. Paul knows good theology will make for good practice.

Paul continues in his bewilderment, asking, "How can we who died to sin still live in it?" (Romans 6:2). For Paul there is something inconsistent, even impossible, about being a believer in Christ and happily persisting in sin. That's why he uses the word "*how*." He does not see how the two things could go together. Why is that? Because for Paul, believing in Christ essentially includes being one who has "died to sin." So saying *a believer* is living in sin is the same thing as saying *a person who has died to sin* is living in sin. Do you see the problem? How could that work? It just doesn't make sense. The two things are incompatible. It's almost a contradiction within the sentence. If we are people who "died to sin," it is impossible that we could also be people who continually live in sin.

Paul backs up his belief that everyone who knows the salvation of Jesus has indeed "died to sin." Again, he anticipates our confusion and asks,

"Do you not know that all of us who have been baptized into Christ Jesus were baptized into his death?" (Romans 6:3). He is essentially saying, "Don't you know that by getting baptized as a believer in Christ you also shared in his death on the cross?" When we believe in Christ, we are mystically unified to him, so that when he died on the cross, it is also as if we died on the cross. Even more so, not only are believers unified to Christ in his death, but in his resurrection! "For if we have been united with him in a death like his, we shall certainly be united with him in a resurrection like his" (Romans 6:5). This means that our confession of faith and the baptism that represents that faith is more than just the forgiveness of our sins, it is also *the merging of our identity with Christ's identity* so much so that his death is like our death and his resurrection is like our resurrection. Through faith we are "in Christ" so that it is as if what happened to Christ has happened to us, and therefore, "We know that our old self was crucified with him" on the cross (Romans 6:6). Is Paul saying that we hung on the cross? By no means! He is saying that Christ dying on the cross is equivalent to saying that your old, sinful self died on the cross. Your old self died *with* Christ. And all the more, your new self came back to life *with* Christ. For Paul, Christ's life, death, and resurrection become the determining factor in our identity.

So how ought the Christian think of herself? "So you also must *consider yourselves* dead to sin and alive to God *in* Christ Jesus" (Romans 6:11). Paul makes an identity statement here. He is making a claim on how we ought to consider ourselves. In other words, he tells us how we should see ourselves, esteem ourselves, and understand ourselves. We

are to do all these things "*in* Christ." The believer's identity ought
to be completely dependent on and wrapped up in the person and
work of Jesus Christ. We only can "consider" ourselves "in Christ."
Indeed, we cannot consider ourselves any other way. Our identity is
dominated by Christ's identity. Our mental health is not the source
of identity. Our opinions are not the source of identity. Our feelings
are not the source of identity. Others' opinions and feelings are not
the source of identity.

Jesus controls our identity.

This theology explains why Paul says things like, "Therefore, if anyone
is in Christ, he is a new creation. The old has passed away; behold,
the new has come" (2 Corinthians 5:17). Being in Christ includes a
change of identity. Who we are "*in*" determines who we "*are*." If we
are "*in*" Christ, then we "*are*" a new creation; therefore, when the
Christian goes to think about herself, she cannot do so apart from
Jesus. Her identity is received from his death and resurrection. To
leave that out would be to leave her without an identity. Believing in
the gospel of Christ is much more than a get-out-of-hell-free-card; it
is a total shift of identity. And for Paul, that is the key doctrine that
will help us fight our inclination towards sin. If we understand our old
self as crucified, and our new self as alive to God (just as Jesus is dead
to sin and alive to God), then we can fight our sin. Good Christian
living depends on a robust understanding of Christian identity.

This may not sound revolutionary at first, but when we consider our
culture's common approach to identity (and identity confusion) we

find an important non-biblical assumption in our society: you can determine who you are. As we have noted, this was the original lie that led Adam and Eve to forfeit paradise. They thought they had the power to make themselves something they were not. But what Paul is teaching us here is that *there is only One Person who has the power to make you something you are not: Jesus Christ.* We live in a society that does not want anyone to have the power to tell us who to be except ourselves. But Paul finds no problem in letting someone else determine his identity. For if Christ did not transform his identity, he would be doomed. And so he is not angry at the oppressive Jesus who makes him be something that he is not. Rather, he is astonished at the kindness of Jesus who empowers him to be something he is not. Jesus makes it possible for Paul to be something far better than he could ever be on his own because of his sin. Asserting your independence from Christ will not give you freedom from the grips of sin. Asserting your *dependence* on Christ will give you freedom from the grips of sin.

Therefore, the cure for identity confusion is not to look inward and try to release your "authentic self" that your society, your family, or your church has suppressed all these years. Rather, we will only find our true identity when we look outside of ourselves. As said so many times throughout this devotional, the Christian identity is a selfless identity, not a self-love identity. Christian identity is a dependent identity: dependent on the person of Christ. It is not the triumph of independence and complete freedom to be whoever we want to be. Because if you ever want to truly obtain a biblical sense of self, you will ultimately have to get past yourself and move on to Christ. You must eventually cease to be continually looking inward and begin looking outward. Your identity is completely dependent on who Jesus is, not who you feel you are, not who you used to be, and not whoever other people tell you that you are supposed to be. You must realize that the Christian finds herself when she loses herself and finds Christ. Similarly, the Christian can only truly consider herself when she first considers Christ.

REFLECTION & APPLICATION:

1. What is the connection between believing in Jesus as your Savior and getting a new sense of self? Why does Paul see the two as intertwined?

2. Do you ever wish you could be someone you are not? Do you ever try to accomplish that on your own? Who has the power to make you into someone you could have never been on your own? What is the determining factor in your identity?

3. How does Paul think identity helps us fight sin? According to Romans 6:1-14, how does a shift in identity (how we "consider" ourselves) affect our daily living?

Self.
DENIAL

What They

TELL YOU:

"Self-care is not self-indulgence, it is self-preservation."

READ MATTHEW 16

What God

TELLS YOU:

"Then Jesus told his disciples, "If anyone would come after me, let him deny himself and take up his cross and follow me. For whoever would save his life will lose it, but whoever loses his life for my sake will find it."

MATTHEW 16:24-25

A s Jesus and his disciples make their way into Caesarea Philippi, Jesus confronts them with a pop quiz: "Who do people say that the Son of Man is?" (Matthew 16:13). The men rattle off a list of the popular opinions of that time, "Some say John the Baptist, others say Elijah, and others Jeremiah or one of the prophets" (Matthew 16:14). Then Jesus presses further, "But who do you say that I am?" (Matthew 16:15). Jesus has referred to himself as the Son of Man throughout his ministry, a title taken from the Old Testament that is associated with an exalted kingly figure in redemptive history (Daniel 7). For those who knew their Old Testament, Jesus identifying himself with the Son of Man was a huge claim. When he inquires about the identity of the Son of Man to his disciples, he's asking about *himself*. He wants to hear the disciples' consensus on his identity. Who is he? Is *he* the Son of Man? Who did they think he actually was? To this, in a rare moment of wisdom, Peter answers, "You are the Christ, the Son of the living God" (Matthew 16:16). Jesus goes on to bless Peter and foretell his role as the rock of the church of Christ.

It is from this key moment forward that "Jesus began to show his disciples that he must go to Jerusalem and suffer many things from the elders and chief priests and scribes, and be killed, and on the third day be raised" (Matthew 16:21). Now that the disciples were clear that he was in fact the Promised Savior King of the Old Testament Scriptures, Jesus needed to ensure they understand what this will really entail. Being aware of the popular misconceptions about the Messiah, he tells them to not spread the news quite yet. Clearly, Jesus was right to assume their susceptibility to such misconceptions because directly following Peter's glorious declaration of Jesus' messiahship, he pulled Jesus aside to rebuke him concerning this crazy talk of persecution and death, saying, "Far be it from you, Lord! This shall never happen to you" (Matthew 16:22). Peter's belief in Jesus as the Christ was fogged by the cultural expectations of his day so much so that he had the audacity to rebuke his Master, the very Master he just proclaimed to be the Christ! Peter was too offended at the idea of a crucified Christ to let this kind of talk slide. A suffering Messiah was an oxymoron to him— incomprehensible. It just could not be. Jesus' response to Peter's rebuke is surprisingly harsh: "Get behind me, Satan!" (Matthew 16:23). He just called Peter "Satan!" In what way had Peter messed with demonic forces? He wanted to change the nature of salvation and the mission of the Messiah. He wanted atonement with no cross. He wanted propitiation with no punishment. *He wanted a win with no loss.* But to distract Jesus from the mission for which he came was to play the role of the devil, and Jesus would have none of it.

It is in this context we hear Jesus' teaching that "If anyone would come after me, let him deny himself and take up his cross and follow me. For whoever would save his life will lose it, but whoever loses his life for my sake will find it" (Matthew 16:24-25). Jesus gives this hard word in response to Peter's arrogant insistence on a certain kind of gospel, more specifically, an easier gospel. Jesus wants to make something clear: if you want to follow *me*, you will have to do it *my* way. In other words, Christ is about to start walking towards Jerusalem to lay down his life. If you can't go there too, you simply cannot follow him. If you want to be a disciple of the One who denied himself and took up his cross, then you need to be willing to follow in his footsteps. Jesus would not allow his followers to be deceived about his messiahship and their discipleship. They could not claim Jesus as Christ and simply go on with life as is. When Jesus hears Peter's profession of faith, he immediately clarifies what it will mean that he is the Messiah so that Peter will know what it means to follow that Messiah. The way of Christ paves the way for the disciples. If Jesus is willing to lose in order to win, they too must be willing to lose in order to win. Jesus is warning his people of the cost of discipleship.

This loaded saying of Jesus is worth serious meditation. What does it mean to deny yourself? What does it mean to take up your cross? What does it mean to lose your life for his sake? It is fairly clear what it would mean to deny oneself. To deny is to reject, disown, or disregard. Jesus said that this ought to be how we treat ourselves. He sets up an ethical system based on self-denial. Jesus did not always grant himself his personal desires and preferences; and therefore, the one who follows him should learn to deny herself similarly. Self-gratification is not the way of Jesus; and therefore, it ought not be the way of his followers. The call to take up one's cross is less clear. Is Jesus asking all of us to die on the cross? This can't be. We have no record of the apostles teaching such a thing, nor evidence that they all died on a cross (though many were likely martyred in other ways). So "carrying" your cross does not mean dying on a cross.

It may help us to understand exactly what it meant at that time to carry your cross. This was a process of public humiliation. It was the official civic designation and display of a condemned criminal to shame them before they received their punishment. It was a legal form of disgrace and denigration. It was a road of suffering that would ultimately lead to death. So for the disciples, being willing to take up their cross meant they were willing to bear the disgrace that might come with the gospel, just as Jesus was. The disciples needed to be prepared for public humiliation, for they would indeed face it soon. And that leads us to Jesus' last call to discipleship: to lose one's life. While Jesus is not saying that every believer will be martyred for the gospel, he is saying that whoever follows in his footsteps must be willing to give in order to receive. They must understand that in "losing," there is "finding."

It is important to note here that there certainly is use of hyperbole in Jesus' statements. This is not to water down Jesus' teaching, not at all. This is just to interpret the text well. Jesus used pithy statements, parables, and proverbial sayings to give his disciples memorable pieces of teaching. Jesus was a Rabbi in an oral culture. Therefore, in order for his disciples to remember the thrust of his teaching, Jesus (as any smart rabbi would) uses figurative, hyperbolic, symbolic, and even outrageous language to get his point across. These are words that the disciples would remember. They make an unforgettable impression. And the overall meaning is certainly clear: following Jesus is not easy. It requires sacrifice and even suffering. Jesus wants the disciples to realize what they're getting themselves into before rushing into discipleship. Being a follower of Jesus means a thoroughly selfless life, and if the disciples did not like that, they could not follow the footsteps of their Rabbi. Jesus uses these poetic, pithy sayings to get that point across. It does not mean we all must literally carry a cross and be martyred for the faith, but it does mean that anyone who seriously considers the call to follow Christ must be willing to deny themselves.

It is easy to see how self-care and self-denial are inherently incompatible. And if this teaching on self-denial was offensive to Peter's ears, it is likely even more offensive to our modern ears. The Western life motto is "treat yourself," not "deny yourself." The trend of self-care is a clear offspring of the self-love gospel in which we believe that salvation comes through loving, embracing, pampering, and celebrating our bodies and our souls. We are constantly bombarded with the message that "If you don't care for yourself, no one else will," and therefore, are often encouraged to resist caring for others because, "Saying yes to others is saying no to yourself. Never say 'no' to yourself!" It is interesting that such ideas have made their way into

Christian thinking without too much resistance. Clearly, the self-care messiah is nothing like the man carrying his cross 2,000 years ago.

So what does this mean for us? Does it mean we should never give ourselves nice things? Does it mean that we must deny our every desire? Does it mean we should not take care of ourselves? Does it mean that we should basically just be miserable? No. Remember, Jesus is using hyperbolic language to help us remember the overall attitude of discipleship. The mindset that pervades our life cannot be self-care. Yes, it does mean we ought to learn to deny ourselves, but it does not mean we can never enjoy nice things. Jesus attended weddings and turned their water into wine! Paul the Apostle spoke to the rich people within Timothy's church and warned them not to set their hope on riches but to enjoy them because God "richly provides us with everything to enjoy" (1 Timothy 6:17). Enjoying nice things is not off limits. So, how can we take Jesus' call to deny ourselves seriously? We must realize that if we always choose to indulge instead of deny, we aren't following Christ. Self-denial is a way of life that says, "It is good sometimes to do things you don't want to do. And it is good to not do things you do want to do." In place of a life focused on self-care and self-indulgence, the Bible offers a different way of healthy living through the Sabbath. God had ordained an order of work and rest that would properly care for his people as they worked and served throughout the week. Jesus is not saying you can never rest. Indeed, when we rest, we mimic our God as he rested in delight after creating the world. The Christian who is concerned about how to care well for themselves should take more time understanding the biblical concept of Sabbath, instead of reading self-care tips. Jesus' words do not need to be applied universally in every situation, but we do need to take self-denial seriously, lest we be like Peter and reject Christ's selfless life and death.

Finally, we must not forget that Jesus does not preach the cost of discipleship without reward. He preaches such a high cost because it is worth it. He says, "Whoever loses his life for my sake *will find it*" (Matthew 16:25). There is a paradox here. The one who supposedly abandons self-interest actually finds self-fulfillment. When they "lose" their life, they "find" their life. It's not all bad news here. There is gain in the midst of the loss—a greater gain than we can imagine. Paul says it best, "But whatever gain I had, I counted as loss for the sake of Christ. Indeed, I count everything as loss because of the surpassing worth of knowing Christ Jesus my Lord. For his sake I have suffered the loss of all things and count them as rubbish, in order that I may gain Christ and be found in him" (Philippians 3:7-9). Jesus takes away only to give us something better. A life of self-denial is never a life of self-loathe nor self-harm. It is a life of self-discipline that is confident that Jesus is always way better than anything we give up.

REFLECTION & APPLICATION:

1. *What does it mean to "deny yourself" and to "take up your cross"? How do we interpret these sayings of Jesus well?*

2. *How can we "deny ourselves" while also recognizing Paul's statement that God gives us good things to enjoy?*

3. *How does Jesus' idea of discipleship contradict our culture's emphasis on self-care?*

HUMILITY

What They

TELL YOU:

"Be enough for yourself first; the rest of the world can wait."

READ PHILIPPIANS 2

What God

TELLS YOU:

"Do nothing from selfish ambition or conceit, but in humility count others more significant than yourselves. Let each of you look not only to his own interests, but also to the interests of others."

PHILIPPIANS 2:3-4

After a heartfelt greeting and introduction, Paul wastes no time to jump into the major section of instruction in his letter to the Philippian church. He begins the letter by saying, "Only let your manner of life be worthy of the gospel of Christ" (Philippians 1:27). This is the call that drives the rest of the section. Though they were not worthy of their salvation in Christ, now that they received it, Paul calls the church to strive to live lives worthy of such a gracious gospel. His command in chapter 2 is a practical application of what a "life worthy of the gospel" looks like. When he says, "So if there is any encouragement in Christ, any comfort from love, any participation in the Spirit, any affection and sympathy" (Philippians 2:1), Paul is essentially saying, "If you have had any encounter with the gospel of Christ this is what you ought to do. If Jesus has had any impact on you at all, you would do this." This is how they can live in a manner worthy of their encounter with the gospel: "Do nothing from selfish ambition or conceit, but in humility count others more significant than yourselves. Let each of you look not only to his own interests, but also to the interests of others" (Philippians 2:3-4). A life worthy of the gospel of Christ is a selfless life because the gospel of Christ is a selfless gospel. If we truly have encountered that gospel, we are compelled to follow suit. We are called away from selfishness and into humility. Paul goes on to explain that this mindset is the very mindset of Christ himself, who, "though he was in the form of God, did not count equality with God a thing to be grasped, but emptied himself, by taking the form of a servant" (Philippians 2:6-7). Christ is the prototype for Christian living. By following in his footsteps, we begin to live in a manner worthy of his gospel.

It is important that we understand exactly what this command to humility entails. Humility is a concept that is becoming increasingly foreign to a society that is obsessed with a certain vision of empowerment. Biblical humility begins to look a lot more like oppression than it does freedom when we have our modern glasses on. We will need to take off our cultural lenses and adjust our focus to understand the beauty of biblical humility. We also have to trust God that his ways are better than our ways, even when it appears not so to us.

The best way to understand the virtue of humility is to see what the text associates it with. First, it is contrasted with selfish ambition and conceit. These two terms are offspring of the vice of pride. The Greek word translated "selfish ambition" has to do with rivalry; and therefore, with a desire to win and for others to lose. It refers to a self-interest including the disregard of our triumph over another. It is often used in the context of competition or division. The Greek word translated "conceit" is more literally "vainglory." The word glory, transliterated "doxa," indicates praise, honor, renown, or high repute. The word vain, "kenos," indicates emptiness, worthlessness, or foolishness. When combined, these terms refer to a type of recognition that serves arrogance and is ultimately futile. To pursue vainglory is to pursue praise and approval just for the sake of pumping up your ego. It is a sinful distortion of true glory. Both of these terms get at the essence of vicious pride. Pride is the disposition which sets others in terms of competition and rank against us. It is a self-centered point of view on life. Other people are not only your competitors, but are objects that you can use to boost your ego. Pride looks for self-exaltation in the wrong places. It is obsessed with receiving approval and applause from others. So if humility is contrasted with an arrogant bend towards attention and reputation, then it makes sense that humility entails "count[ing] others more significant than yourselves. Let[ting] each of you look not only to his own interests, but also to the interests of others" (Philippians 2:3-4).

While selfish ambition views others in terms of rivalry, *humility regards others as more important than one's self*. While conceit seeks out one's own interest and praise, humility seeks out the interests and glory of another. We tend to think of humility in terms of self-esteem or a way of thinking of oneself, but Paul associates it with a way of thinking of others. Paul's vision of humility has less to do with what we think about ourselves and more to do with how we think about others. Humility is more about the *priority* of others rather than the *superiority* of others; therefore, it does not insist that we think of ourselves as inferior. Paul does not command them to think poorly of themselves. He does not really say much about self-image; he simply says to think more about others. This is made all the more clear when he applies humility to Christ. Certainly, Christ did not think poorly of himself, so that cannot be the essence of humility. Rather, Christ, knowing his identity as God (a very high view of his identity!), nonetheless gives his life to the good and interest of others. Humility and greatness can go hand and hand. In fact, the greater a person is, the more impressive their humility becomes. That is why Christ's humility will always surpass ours. Because not only does he care more about other people than we do, but he is much more worthy of his own self-love than we are. His commitment to the other is all the more praiseworthy because he is himself so great that you might think he wouldn't bother with us. Christ was equal with God, but he did not use that to assert himself over others. His position of superiority was not used for his agenda; instead, he gave up a position of authority and became a servant.

It becomes clear that although pride is often mixed with a high sense of self, humility is not necessarily connected to a low sense of self. Humility is more about emphasis than it is about rank. Selfish ambition, rivalry, conceit, and vainglory are all obsessed with being evaluated over and against other people a certain way. Self-esteem (how we see ourselves) becomes the center of being, but the humble person is less concerned about how she ranks in comparison to others and is more concerned about the other. It is not a change from high to low self-esteem; it is a change from self-esteem to esteeming others.

It is about focus. It is about priority. Pride focuses on the self and prioritizes the self. Humility focuses on the other and prioritizes the other. Arrogance is often accompanied by self-absorption, just as humility is often accompanied by self-forgetfulness. When it comes to self-evaluation, the humble person esteems herself with sober judgment; not self-exalting nor self-deprecating. A humble person can see herself as she truly is rather than pretending to be better or worse. But the major difference between the humble person and the proud person is not just that the humble person esteems herself correctly, but it is that self-esteem is not at the heart of her being like it is for the proud person. She is not consumed with esteeming herself; rather, she is consumed with esteeming others. She is not captivated by considering herself, but is captivated with the consideration of others.

Personal empowerment, meaning the freedom and confidence to do what you want, has become the cry of today's culture. Society's popular vision of empowerment is the freedom to assert yourself. It is the confidence to stand up for yourself. It is the bravery to fight for yourself. The heroes of empowerment are those who are willing to prioritize themselves. But the biblical sense of humility is utterly incompatible with such a worldview and view of the self. Autonomy, the ability to assert oneself, is the very privilege Jesus enjoyed as God, and yet also the very privilege he laid aside and instead became a servant of others, even being obedient unto death (Philippians 2:8). Empowerment in our world means we are completely self-assured, confident, and never held back by others. Empowerment, in the biblical world, means we are completely others-oriented and often called to sacrifice our own interests for the interests of others. And so the biblically empowered woman embodies humility. She is not obsessed with self-image, rank, or interests. She prioritizes the people around her, counting them more significant than herself; she does this not because she hates herself or does not appreciate herself, she does it because that's what Jesus did.

REFLECTION **&** APPLICATION:

1. *Does being prideful always mean you are arrogant and think too highly of yourself? If so, why does the Bible assign pride to all of humanity? There are plenty of people that think horribly of themselves. How, under the true definition of pride, can a person with really low self-esteem still struggle with the sin of pride?*

2. *Does being humble always mean you think badly or lowly of yourself? Does humility mean that you hate yourself and never appreciate yourself? If humility equals low self-esteem, how was Jesus humble? Define humility the way Paul does.*

3. *How can you "count others as more significant than yourself" in your daily life? Come up with three concrete ways you could do this.*

SERVICE

What They

TELL YOU:

"Be brave enough to prioritize yourself."

READ MARK 10

What God

TELLS YOU:

"But whoever would be great among you must be your servant, and whoever would be first among you must be slave of all. For even the Son of Man came not to be served but to serve, and to give his life as a ransom for many."

MARK 10:43-45

In Mark 10, James and John, the pair of brothers within the twelve disciples, present quite the request before their Rabbi: "Grant us to sit, one at your right hand and one at your left, in your glory" (Mark 10:37). As we would expect, Jesus is not thrilled with their presumption. While they are busy thinking about who will get to sit next to Jesus on a shiny throne, Jesus proclaims to them the reality of his coming humiliation and death (Mark 10:32-34). Revealing their ignorance, he asks if they are willing to "drink the cup" he is about to drink (Mark 10:38). This clearly refers to the few verses that come before this text that speak of Jesus' crucifixion. In foolish confidence, not realizing what they are committing to, they say "We are able," but Jesus is not satisfied. Their request is denied.

When the rumors spread around the rest of the group about James and John's little meeting with Jesus, the other ten disciples were upset. So, Jesus decides to offer a bit of wisdom they all really need to hear. Despite his straightforward declaration of his coming death, the disciples still don't seem to get the nature of Jesus' mission as the Messiah. His position of glory and authority took a path unlike worldly rulers and kings. He explains, "You know that those who are considered rulers of the Gentiles lord it over them, and their great ones exercise authority over them. *But it shall not be so among you.* But whoever would be great among you must be your servant, and whoever would be first among you must be slave of all" (Mark 10:42-44). James and John had a vision of leadership like that of the Gentiles (the non-Jewish community). But Jesus flips greatness and leadership on its head. The disciples are hungry for glory and power, and therefore, are just like their non-believing counterparts. If they truly want to be disciples—followers of Jesus—they have to follow his paradigm of greatness: "For even the Son of Man came not to be served but to serve, and to give his life as a ransom for many" (Mark 10:45).

The disciples could not seem to get it through their thick skulls that Jesus was far different than the world around him. Their assumptions about messiahship and glory completely excluded a crucial part of Jesus' ministry: his work as a servant. The essence of Jesus' earthly leadership was servanthood, and they could not grasp such a paradox. To them, being great and being a servant simply didn't go together. That insistence remains in the modern imagination. But if the greatest man on earth oriented his life towards the service of others, certainly his inferior disciples ought to do the same.

Indeed, after Jesus washes his disciples' feet, an act of humility and subjection, he tells his disciples, "If I then, your Lord and Teacher, have washed your feet, you also ought to wash one another's feet. For

I have given you an example, that you also should do just as I have done to you. Truly, truly, I say to you, a servant is not greater than his master, nor is a messenger greater than the one who sent him. If you know these things, blessed are you if you do them" (John 13:14-17).

This reversal of values continues to be unappealing to Christ's followers today. We too are offended at the idea of enslavement. Servitude is not a lifestyle we are interested in—that has oppression written all over it. Without even realizing it, we tend to see the world through Marx-colored glasses, always viewing society in terms of the oppressed and the powerful. And our cultural tendency towards victimhood means we like to take the position of the oppressed. We are inclined to view ourselves as the victim that needs to be freed and empowered, and therefore, we are completely disgusted that Jesus would affirm such an oppressed status as servanthood.

Salvation, in this Marxist sense, is all about the overthrow of oppression. And so it is today. We think of salvation in terms of empowerment. The epitome of virtue and authenticity is throwing off society's oppressive standards and doing whatever makes you happy. And with minds so repulsed by the idea of being controlled, we cannot embrace the full essence of servant leadership as seen in Christ. We don't mind doing favors for friends, and of course we are all about "love," but that love is a love that starts with loving ourselves. So living a life completely oriented towards serving the needs and desires of other people, especially people who aren't kind to you, is self-demeaning. It is letting the patriarchy control you. It is letting others make your choices for you. The role of servanthood is degrading. In a very similar way, the disciples of Jesus were appalled at his model of leadership. They too thought of salvation in terms of worldly empowerment. For them, empowerment meant getting a throne right next to Jesus. For us, empowerment means asserting and prioritizing ourselves. Neither understanding of empowerment seems to recognize that it is the humble who will be exalted. It was only because Christ "humbled himself by becoming obedient to the point of death, even death on a cross" that God "highly exalted him and bestowed on him the name that is above every name" (Philippians 2:8-9).

The road to empowerment is the road of submission. The path to exaltation starts first at humiliation. The way to greatness was first a commitment to servanthood. If we take the life of Christ seriously, we must first acknowledge that a life built on self-service is not a Christian life. It is quite troubling that many young people in the church have not noticed how the self-care movement can often be the direct antithesis of the Christian life. Surely the Christ follower should take showers, take proper rest, and tend to their physical needs. But the idea of prioritizing your needs, your happiness, and your dreams is anti-gospel. And sadly, it is that simple.

The Christian is *certainly* not to live a life of self-harm. Christ never harmed himself. But that does not necessarily mean the Christian is to live a life of so-called "self-care." When we look at the life of Christ, we notice he took time alone (Mark 6:46), invested in his own personal spirituality (Luke 5:16), took care of his physical needs

(Matthew 11:19), and participated in the weekly Sabbath rest as was standard in his Jewish upbringing (Luke 4:16). But we also see that his life's mission is completely others-oriented. His self-care was not a way to "treat himself;" it was proper stewardship of his body and spirit. His life is marked by a servanthood that is primarily concerned with the needs of others. Service is a matter of priority. Self-care is a secondary responsibility in order that he might serve well. And that cannot be disputed using scriptural evidence. If self-care is the most urgent need of the human self, why do the Gospels not reflect that need? It is only when we read our desires into the text that we can find self-care as an emphasis in the New Testament.

The proper application of Jesus' words to his disciples in Mark 10 is to not seek out empowerment, but to seek out servitude. The emptiness and confusion within ourselves is due to the fact that we have not taken upon ourselves the mindset of Christ which sought to serve others and expected nothing in return. He was only confident in God's blessing of him in doing so. The proper application of this text is not to stop sleeping, eating, and combing your hair. It simply means that life should not be about serving yourself; it's about serving others. Your mission is not to be served, but to serve—just like it was for your Master. When we live a life of servanthood, we reflect God's image the way we were meant to. We become who we were meant to be. Service is empowering.

When you are struggling with identity, Jesus says that serving others is a great way to help. Go out and help those in need. Focus on giving and not so much on receiving. And when it feels like the opposite of empowering and more like belittling, let us have the faith of Christ that looks beyond this world to the reward on the other side. We can be "looking to Jesus, the founder and perfecter of our faith, who for the joy that was set before him endured the cross, despising the shame, and is seated at the right hand of the throne of God. Consider him who endured from sinners such hostility against himself, so that you may not grow weary or fainthearted." (Hebrews 12:2-3). For the joy that is set before us, may we endure a life of service, even when it's hard.

REFLECTION **&** APPLICATION:

1. *Sometimes being a servant makes us feel like a doormat; it can make us feel like people are using us. How, then, could servanthood help us with our identity? It seems more like it would hurt us.*

2. *Jesus' mission was to serve others, to give himself up for others, but we know Jesus also took care of himself properly. So how do we balance a servant mindset with a healthy mindset of self-care? In other words, how do we make sure servanthood is our main priority while never neglecting to take care of our bodies and souls?*

3. *Is servanthood the final word for Jesus? Will it be the final word for those who follow him? Notice that in Mark 10 that Jesus uses the phrase "whoever would be great among you...." Are servanthood and greatness opposites?*

The End of
THE MATTER

What They

TELL YOU:

"You will only love yourself once you stop demanding so much from yourself."

READ LUKE 10:25-42

What God

TELLS YOU:

"The end of the matter; all has been heard. Fear God and keep his commandments, for this is the whole duty of man. For God will bring every deed into judgment, with every secret thing, whether good or evil."

ECCLESIASTES 12:13-14

The book of Ecclesiastes grapples with the confusion and despair we confront when we consider the state of our world. If you have ever been at a loss when it comes to understanding this messed up world, the book of the Ecclesiastes ought to be somewhat of a comfort to you. You are not alone. Even God's Word acknowledges that our world is quite the enigma. It is often an evil mystery we cannot fully grasp—a "chasing after wind." And while the book of Ecclesiastes gives space for our disorientation and frustration when looking at the world, it does leave us with a way to live in the midst of the chaos. After chapters of turmoil and despondency, the book finishes: "The end of the matter; all has been heard. Fear God and keep his commandments, for this is the whole duty of man. For God will bring every deed into judgment, with every secret thing, whether good or evil" (Ecclesiastes 12:13-14). Despite the author's sober recognition that the world is an awfully confusing and frustrating place to be, he acknowledges that he is nonetheless obligated to live a certain way. He was still responsible to fear God and to keep his commandments. It seems to me that this is the proper ending reflection for our study.

You may be walking away from this book overwhelmed by its claims about culture, the self, and how we ought to respond and live amidst all of that. There's a lot to consider. It may seem like too complex and burdensome of a task. The road towards secure Christian identity may seem like a long, winding path through a dark and dense forest. The number of things that need to be addressed accumulate to a pile too high to even approach. It may take you and me the rest of our lives to even partially apply the truths we have considered in the past six weeks. Understanding ourselves in light of gospel truths can be quite an intimidating task. So, if you are feeling overwhelmed, over-stimulated, weary, incapable, or discouraged, hear these final words of wisdom from Ecclesiastes: "Fear God and keep his commandments." That is your full duty. Commit yourself to doing this more and more, day by day, and you will begin to embrace the truths you've learned about Christian identity.

Fear of God is a posture of the heart that has encountered God's grandeur. Sometimes this leads to a true moment of terror or dread. The power, justice, and holiness of God can be downright frightening. But fear of the Lord also includes a fear that denotes reverence and worship. Because of the work of Christ, we do not have to tremble in fear before God because he might condemn or harm us; rather, we tremble before God in awe of his scandalous grace and love in Christ

Jesus, completely overwhelmed by his goodness and worthiness. This is the spiritual disposition we are to strive for as a Christian.

The way we grow in fear of the Lord is through the basics of worship: reading his Word, praying, and participating in the local church community through worship and service. And, as the text suggests, the practical outworking of fear of the Lord is obedience. So as we grow in fear of God, we will begin to obey more and more. His commandments will become our delight and honor. This task is not incredibly complicated nor complex. It is fairly simple. These two commands—to fear God and keep his commandments—are parallel to Jesus' statement that life is all about loving God and loving others. The fear of God is ultimately the true love of God. And the commandment of God is to love your neighbor. So if you want to fear God and keep his commandments, start by loving God and loving your neighbor. That's not too confusing. You've got that!

Continue to grapple with the lies that enter your mind concerning who you are now and who you were made to be. But never let the conversation of identity dominate your faith. Secure identity is not the center of the gospel. Remember what Paul delivered to the church of Corinth "of first importance": "that Christ died for our sins in accordance with the Scriptures, that he was buried, that he was raised on the third day in accordance with the Scriptures" (1 Corinthians 15:3-4). That is what you must preach to yourself every morning. And with such a great God that would love a sinner to the point of death, it only makes sense that this Good News of first importance would foster in us a fear of God and desire to keep his commandments, which is the "whole duty of man" (Ecclesiastes 12:13). That is your duty. And you can accomplish that duty by making the main thing the main thing. The daily struggle does not need to be a struggle of identity and self image. That's not the main thing (though it is certainly an important thing). The main thing is the gospel and the main duty is to love God and love your neighbor. Make sure the main thing stays the main thing, and you will be surprised at the progress you make in your sense of identity.

Mary sat herself at the feet of Jesus. She must have been completely captivated by the teaching and wisdom of her Master. In a culture where only men were privileged to be trained by Rabbis, Jesus welcomed Mary to sit at his feet and learn alongside the men. She was hungry to learn, and he was ready to provide. But her sister Martha was flustered in the other room preparing food and serving. She asks Jesus, "Lord, do you not care that my sister has left me to serve alone? Tell her then to help me" (Luke 10:40). But Jesus answers Martha with words worth our careful meditation: "Martha, Martha, you are anxious and troubled about many things, but one thing is necessary. Mary has chosen the good portion, which will not be taken away from her" (Luke 10:41-42). We live in an anxious age. We are indeed anxious and troubled about many things, our identity is just one among the many obstacles in our life that trouble us. Hear the words of Jesus: keep the main thing the main thing. Mary knew the main thing that day, and she chose to focus on it. Do not let the conversation in your head keep you from sitting at the feet of your

Master, desperate to know him better. Choose the good portion, and it will not be taken away from you.

I could end this book by giving you a pep talk about your capability to accomplish whatever you want to. I could hype you up and tell you how strong you are. I could remind you that "You are enough," but that would directly contradict my entire book. Nonetheless, I am confident in you. Not because you are capable. Not because you are strong. Not because you are enough. But because "he who is in you is greater than he who is in the world" (1 John 4:4). You will overcome, and that's not a wishy-washy form of wishful thinking. It is a certainty in the ability of God to do what he said he would do. By his Spirit, you *can* do this. Go get 'em.

REFLECTION & APPLICATION:

1. *In the face of confusion and overstimulation, what is the simple conclusion in the book of Eccelesiastes?*

2. *What is the full duty of man? How is Jesus' command to love God and love our neighbor essentially the same duty described in Ecclesiastes? How is that duty fueled by knowing and embracing the gospel?*

3. *What is the "main thing" in the Christian life? How can you keep it the main thing?*

"Now to him who is able to do far more abundantly than all that we ask or think, according to the power at work within us, to him be glory in the church and in Christ Jesus throughout all generations, forever and ever. Amen."

EPHESIANS 3:20-21